Practical Buddhism

Practical Buddhism

Mindfulness and Skilful Living in the Modern Era

Paramabandhu Groves

Muswell Hill Press

First published by Muswell Hill Press, London, 2013

© 2013 Paramabandhu Groves

Paramabandhu Groves has asserted his right under the Copyright, Design and Patents Act 1988 to be identified as the author of this work. All rights reserved. No part of this publication may be reproduced without prior permission of Muswell Hill Press.

www.muswellhillpress.co.uk.

British Library Cataloguing in Publication Data

A C.I.P. for this title is available from the British Library

ISBN-13: 978-1-908995-03-2

Printed and bound in Great Britain

For Joan and Len

Contents

Acknowledgments

Many thanks to Tim Read, who has patiently and skilfully guided me through the writing of this book from its inception. Editing from Keiron Le Grice helped to clarify and sharpen the text. I am grateful to Knut Wilmott, Jnanavaca, Todd Donnelly and Glenn Kitsune, who gave useful comments on earlier drafts. Finally, much appreciation goes to my teachers, especially Subhuti and Sangharakshita, who have generously made the Dharma available to me and many others.

PG
February 2013

Foreword

Dr. Sarah Eagger
Consultant psychiatrist, honorary senior lecturer, executive committee member and past chair of the Spirituality and Psychiatry Special Interest Group at the Royal College of Psychiatrists.

When asked what surprised him most about humanity, the Dalai Lama allegedly answered 'Man. Because he sacrifices his health in order to make money. Then he sacrifices money to recuperate his health. And then he is so anxious about the future that he does not enjoy the present; the result being that he does not live in the present or the future; he lives as if he is never going to die, and then dies having never really lived'. This is a good description of the situation many find themselves in today and why people are now turning in increasing numbers to ancient wisdom to help solve the problems of finding contentment in everyday life.

Paramabandhu and I both sought out a spiritual practice while studying at medical school, he in the UK while I was in Australia, but for many years this felt more of a personal journey quite separate from our professional lives. This situation has changed considerably over the years with the existence of several university departments on spirituality and health and, most significantly for us, the setting up of the Spirituality and Psychiatry Special Interest Group at the Royal College of Psychiatrists. This is the professional body for psychiatrists in the UK and the Republic of Ireland. We both sit on the executive committee of this body and have been working, with other members, on ways to make 'the spiritual' understandable to our colleagues and more accessible to those who may derive benefit from its fundamental message and practice.

This special interest group is increasingly influential. The Royal College of Psychiatrists has accepted a position paper which we proposed, advocating a truly holistic model of bio-psycho-social-spiritual mental health. We have also run meditation workshops at the Royal College of Psychiatrists Annual Conference, and been pleasantly surprised at how well attended they have been and the response we received.

Clearly, mindfulness is a practice relevant to both practitioners and service users alike. The National Institute of Clinical Excellence (NICE) recommends Mindfulness-Based Cognitive Therapy for the treatment of anxiety and depression. Much research has been conducted verifying the positive effect of this treatment for many mental health problems. Undoubtedly mindfulness is a buzz word these days — 'mindfulness with everything' — but what does it actually mean and what is the spiritual context from which it has been so fashionably extracted? We are fortunate indeed to have the clear and thoughtful explanations from Dr. Paramabandhu Groves to shed light on these questions.

Paramabandhu is the real thing, a practising psychiatrist and committed Buddhist who has brought together his wisdom from both fields to help us understand what 'all this mindfulness stuff' is about. What are the modern benefits and what are the spiritual and cultural origins? He has patiently, through his own experience and study, developed a profound understanding of these complex ideas and techniques. He helps us to appreciate what these ideas mean in everyday life and clinical practice.

Refreshingly concise and easy to read and digest, this book is peppered with examples and stories as it leads us through the historical background of the Buddha, what is really meant by mindfulness and how this relates to cognitive behavioural therapy. Other areas explored include: what is true kindness, how to cultivate loving kindness, how to meditate and the nature of precepts of Buddhism that guide mindful living. We are all familiar with the phrases such as 'right livelihood', but what does this actually mean? It's really satisfying to get such a clear understanding of how all these Buddhist ideas fit together with psychotherapy and psychological distress. Paramabandhu is clearly pointing to something very fundamental about ourselves, our core essence, but then also expands to take in the wider picture of our struggles with life, death and everything in between. You'll enjoy reading this book — small in size but big on wisdom.

Foreword

Vishvapani Blomfield
*Buddhist writer, broadcaster and teacher, mindfulness
trainer and member of the Triratna Buddhist Order*

The Buddha sometimes likened himself to a physician. He is often described as a religious figure and sometimes as a philosopher; but his own view was that, like a physician, his sole concern was 'suffering and the end of suffering'. His teaching of the Four Noble Truths is founded on a medical model. First, he identifies the disease, which he calls *dukkha* — a Pāli and Sanskrit word meaning all the physical and mental suffering, dis-ease and unsatisfactoriness of our lives. Then he diagnoses the cause of *dukkha*, which he says is craving. Conversely, it follows that the cure for *dukkha* is eradicating craving. And finally, the treatment he prescribes is following the Eightfold Path of right or helpful views, motivations, communication, action, livelihood, effort, awareness and meditation.

This teaching identifies the mind itself as the key to understanding and changing experience; so, updating the Buddha's physician analogy, perhaps we should call him the first, and even the essential, psychologist.

To recover the freshness of the Buddha's contribution it helps to know that his approach was fundamentally different from anything his predecessors or contemporaries had followed in India or elsewhere. The early sources of the Buddha's life tell us that, disillusioned with both worldly existence and the various religious alternatives available to him, he used the concentration and mental pliancy of deep meditation to observe his own mental processes. He discovered that his mind was endlessly malleable: constantly forming itself and reshaping the mould in which future experiences would develop. Difficult states were the result of past responses, especially craving; while different choices would bring different results.

The Buddha's psychological eminence derives from his capacity not only to understand and change himself, but also to generalise his understanding. His principle that 'What we frequently dwell upon and ponder becomes the inclination of our thoughts' was the starting point for a detailed analysis of perceptions, responses and the whole process of mental formation. However, the Buddha's concern was not to understand the mind but to change it. He saw that it matters profoundly which of the many emotions and thoughts that bubble into our experience we pursue and foster. He passionately urged his students to know their motivations, responses, beliefs and emotions and see their effects. And he devised a detailed and subtle methodology for change which he formulated in the Eightfold Path.

The fact that it is still possible to entitle a book *Practical Buddhism* suggests that human experience has not fundamentally changed in the 2,500 years since the Buddha. The ancient Buddhist texts outline fundamental patterns of human experience that anyone can see in their own experience. But society has changed, and applying the Buddha's insights today requires someone with Paramabandhu's experience, understanding and practical focus. He is not alone in seeking to do this. Perhaps the most prevalent form of contemporary *dukkha* is what we term 'stress', and it is no accident that the most successful large-scale application of Buddhist teachings in Western societies is Jon Kabat Zinn's Mindfulness-Based Stress Reduction programme. Other mindfulness-based approaches apply similar techniques to pain management, avoiding depression relapse and a host of other conditions.

Paramabandhu himself teaches Mindfulness-Based Cognitive Therapy and has developed Mindfulness-Based Relapse Prevention for recovering addicts. But what he outlines in this book goes much further than mindfulness-based approaches. Paramabandhu has been practising Buddhism for almost thirty years and teaching it for over twenty, and he knows that mindfulness is only one element of what we need to change. The strong emphasis on kindness in this book reflects both Paramabandhu's character and his style as a teacher; and the chapters on ethics, friendship, livelihood and ritual show the breadth of Buddhist practice. He also shows that the Buddha was far more than a psychologist in the modern, professional sense. For the Buddha, the implications of the mental processes he identified were very profound and our potential for mental change was equally unbounded.

Practical Buddhism is a clear, simple and accessible guide to Buddhist ideas and practices, but beneath that simplicity is a deep understanding of the Buddha's teachings. In Paramabandhu's hands these ancient ideas seem like the freshest of insights and the most *practical* of all methods of personal change.

Introduction

Do not go by oral tradition, by lineage of teaching,
by hearsay, by a collection of texts . . .
by the seeming competence of a speaker,
or because you think, 'The ascetic is our teacher.'
But when you know for yourselves,
'These things are unwholesome; these things are blamable;
these things are censured by the wise;
these things, if undertaken and practised, lead to harm and suffering,'
then you should abandon them.[1]

—The Buddha

I was a medical student on one of my first retreats when I first studied the *Kālāma Sutta*. The Kālāmas were a clan living in remote part of the Ganges basin at the time of the Buddha, who were confused by all the different spiritual teachings around at that time and wanted to know what they could rely on. One teacher would promote one set of ideas, only for the next teacher passing through to debunk them and put forward a different teaching. So when the Buddha visited them, they explained their dilemma and asked him to clarify who was speaking the truth and who was not. The Buddha's response was pragmatic. As quoted above, he replied that you should not go on hearsay or blind belief. The twin tests of all teachings were their effect in your own experience and whether they were commended by the wise.

Back then, I particularly responded to the former criterion. For example, did the teaching, when put into practice, lead to greater happiness and contentment? If it did, it should be engaged in. Or did it lead to harm and suffering? In this case, it should be abandoned. This was the *Dharma*, the Buddha's teaching. I found this refreshing and a relief. Here was a set of teachings that did not rest on something I could not verify. I had to put it into practice and see if it was helpful. The implication was also that anything that could help move you towards inner freedom was the *Dharma* too, even if it was not formally Buddhist. So the teaching was not something that was frozen in time or exclusive to received Buddhist doctrines. If it helps, then use it. As a medical student interested in becoming a psychiatrist, it meant that approaches I might learn in my training, such as psychotherapy, could in principle be included in my practice of the *Dharma*.

As a young man with individualistic leanings — like many of us in the modern Westernized world — it was perhaps not surprising that I responded to the first criterion, but barely noticed the other test: the testimony of the wise. Although the issue of who are the 'wise' is something of a fraught question, over time I have come to see it is an important counterbalance to one-sided individualism. Without the benefit of those more experienced than me on the path, I can be blinded by my own biases. Like learning anything new we can benefit both from putting in effort and monitoring its effects and by being receptive to those with greater experience. Even on that retreat where I was learning the importance of testing the teachings of the Buddha in my own experience, I was also being taught. I was being introduced to this fundamental quality of how to approach Buddhism by the teacher. Inspired by the weekend of study (as would happen many times in the future when I met or was introduced to something in Buddhism I found uplifting), I wanted to put it into practice straight away.

In this book, *Practical Buddhism*, I have tried to show the practical aspects of the Buddha's teaching, to indicate how you can use it in your life to make a real difference. Most of the chapters follow the sort of things you are likely to learn if you were to go to a Buddhist centre in order to put the Buddha's teachings into practice. Often people first go to a Buddhist centre to learn to meditate. So chapters two to four describe meditation, especially practising mindfulness and kindness (you will find a link at the end of the book that can take you to some guided meditations to listen to online or download). Our meditation is affected by what we do in the rest of our lives, just as meditation when practised diligently will affect our life outside of formal meditation. Chapter five looks at Buddhist ethical principles and how to live skilfully in a way that supports our meditation and conduces to our happiness. One of the main contexts that affects how we behave is our work. The theme of our livelihood is taken up in chapter six. Buddhism places great importance on friendship and this is explored in chapter seven. Ritual is an area of practice that complements meditation, although it sometimes comes as surprise to people that it is part of Buddhism. Chapter eight describes ritual and devotion, and its place in Buddhism. There has been a lot of interest by psychotherapists in the Buddha's teachings, particularly meditation. Moreover, many people who are practising Buddhism also seek psychotherapeutic help. As a psychiatrist, who has trained in psychotherapy, it seemed pertinent to address this area (chapter nine). The final chapter explores wisdom, which is a distinctive feature of Buddhism. Wisdom is both the final step that leads directly to enlightenment, the ultimate aim of Buddhism, and a way of talking about the content of the enlightenment experience.

To bring the book to life I have included various vignettes of people practising Buddhism. These are drawn from my experience of practising and teaching Buddhism over more than 20 years. To preserve people's anonymity I haven't described specific individuals.[2] Rather, these are composite, with personal details changed, but I hope they will help to illustrate the sorts of issues that we face when trying to put the Buddha's teaching into practice.

Before we look at how we practise Buddhism, however, it might be helpful to have an idea of who the Buddha was. Chapter one therefore describes the Buddha and his context, and it is to this that we will now turn.

CHAPTER 1

The Buddha in Context

'In a home', thought that man, 'a life is stifled.
For the wanderer, there is space.'
He saw this was so and set off.[1]
　　　　　　　　　　　　　—Pabbajjā Sutta

The earliest account of the quest of Siddhartha Gautama — the man who would become the Buddha — is sparse. Later descriptions are more elaborate, as the story of the early life of the Buddha became mixed with myth and legend. However, both accounts can provide us with food for reflection and point to the inner meanings of the Buddha's journey to awakening. As we will see at the end of this chapter, this deeper significance has profound relevance for us today.

The Historical Context

The Buddha lived in an area corresponding to modern day northern India and some of Nepal, mostly within the Ganges Valley. He was born about 484 BCE into a wealthy family in the province of the Shakyans, which was the name of the clan. His father appears to have been one of the leaders of the clan. At that time there were a number of small states, which were oligarchies or kingdoms. There was considerable rivalry between the states, and over the course of the Buddha's life he would see many of the smaller states — including his own — swallowed up by neighbouring aggressors. After his death the Ganges Valley came under the control of the Maghadan kingdom, which later became the Mauryan Empire that would stretch across much of the Indian subcontinent.[2]

As well as political unrest there was a ferment of spiritual ideas. This was the Axial Age, a period that, across the planet, saw the emergence of some of the first great thinkers and founders of religion such as Plato in Greece, the great prophets in the Middle East, and Confucius in China. The Axial Age marked a significant developmental step in human consciousness characterised by unprecedented self-awareness.[3] These Axial-Age individuals addressed fundamental existential questions such as how we should live and the meaning of life. In India there were broadly two religious groups: *brahmins* who lived in the villages and towns and presided over religious rites such as marriages and funerals, and *shramanas* or wanderers who had gone forth from family life and lived by begging for alms. The *shramanas'* main spiritual activities consisted of practising austerities, meditation and debating philosophical theories.[4] The *brahmins* were the spiritual orthodoxy, basing their views on texts called the Vedas out of which Hinduism developed. The *shramanas* held a wide variety of views, challenging the orthodoxy of the *brahmins*. At the time of the Buddha in India there were a number of prominent figures including Mahāvīra, one of the principal founders of Jainism.[5] Despite the political unrest in the region, there was sufficient wealth to support a large community of wanderers, and giving alms to such a 'holy man' was generally seen to be beneficial in addition to supporting the *brahmins*.

The Four Sights

It is against this backdrop that Siddhartha Gautama was born, became enlightened as the Buddha, and, in teaching the way to enlightenment for others, founded the religion we now call Buddhism.[6] We can understand something of the main aim of Buddhism by contemplating the early life of the Buddha. After his awakening the Buddha described key events in his life that led to him setting out on a spiritual quest. These are called the four sights. Legend has it that at the Buddha's birth it was predicted by a seer that the Buddha would become either a great world leader or a great spiritual being. His father wanted the former and so arranged the Buddha's life to be filled with pleasure and anything unpleasant to be removed. However, rather than this leading to the Buddha wanting to obtain more pleasure, it seemed to create a restlessness, which led him to want to see more of life. It was as if at some level the Buddha knew that pleasure and power could not be ultimately satisfying. He arranged for his charioteer to take him on various excursions from the palace. During these outings he encountered in turns an old person, a sick person, a dead person and then a *shramana*.

The first three sights led to disillusionment with his life in the pursuit of pleasure and the fourth offered a way forward or at least an alternative approach to life. In the first three sights the Buddha came face to face with the existential facts of life: inevitably we all suffer sickness, we will grow old (if we are lucky!) and we will all die. Against this a life led in the pursuit of pleasure or worldly power palled. Coming face to face with the inherent suffering of life sharpened the Buddha's dissatisfaction with life as it is ordinarily lived. The *shramana* tradition was questioning the received wisdom of how life should be lived. With the inquisitiveness and idealism of a youthful mind, the Buddha followed the example of the wanderer in quest of a better solution.

Going Forth

The bare version quoted at the start of this chapter simply has the Buddha experiencing the home life as stifling and contrasting this with the taste of freedom in the outdoor life of a wanderer. Fuller versions describe the Buddha's parents trying to dissuade him from going, his wife in dreams having premonitions of her husband leaving, and the Buddha stealing away in the middle of the night, tearing himself away from his wife and son only with some difficulty. We don't know for sure whether the Buddha really had a wife and son, but the story perhaps points to the internal struggle the Buddha may have undergone in choosing to wholeheartedly follow a spiritual calling. It suggests that the Buddha was facing so great a crisis that it demanded he put aside his love and attachment to what was most dear to him (his wife and son). What is clear, however, is that the Buddha, like many of us, experienced a keen urgency to find answers to the spiritual questions that troubled him.

Taking up the life of a wanderer, initially the Buddha approached the renowned teachers of his day. From them he learnt meditation practices, but these failed to provide him with the answers he was looking for. He then turned to extreme ascetic practices. A prevalent view at the time was that if you mortified the flesh, you would release the spirit and so find freedom. The idea underlying this practice of mortification was that we all have an immortal soul (*ātman*), but this was bound up in the flesh. Ascetic practices were seen as the means to extricate the soul from the body so that it could enter into its natural state. The Buddha pursued ascetic practices, such as not eating, almost to the point of death and developed quite a following, with five particularly close disciples who practised asceticism with him. However, eventually the Buddha conceded that starvation in this way was not taking him any closer to liberation.

The Buddha's Awakening

It is said that the Buddha recalled an event from childhood. He was sitting under a rose-apple tree, watching his father ploughing a field. His father, as an important elder, may have been ritually marking the opening of the season. As he watched his father, he spontaneously entered into a blissful absorbed state. The Buddha realized that he need not be afraid of pleasure, as long as that pleasure was skilful. He intuited that a more balanced approach to his quest, which did not eschew the body in such an extreme way, could take him forward. He started eating again, much to the disgust of his five disciples who promptly left him. With renewed strength from moderate eating, and re-inspired, he found a large pipal tree and took up meditation again.[7] With a balanced and flexible mind, refined through meditation, he reflected on the nature of existence. The Buddha saw deeply into the conditioned, impermanent flux of reality and found liberation. Everywhere he looked he saw change; phenomena arising and passing away in dependence on conditions. In particular, he saw that there was no fixed self or immortal, unchanging *ātman,* as those following ascetic practices believed. He saw that this 'self' was habitually constructed and that belief in and attachment to this 'self' caused suffering. Seeing through this ingrained and tenaciously held notion of a permanently existing self led him to liberation. Thus the Buddha gained what has been variously called awakening, enlightenment or *nirvāṇa*. He became the Buddha — literally, 'one who is awake'. The content of that experience we will explore more fully in the final chapter on wisdom.

The Buddha's Teaching Career

Attaining enlightenment put the Buddha in something of a quandary. On the one hand, he experienced a strong compassionate urge to help others find liberation from suffering. On the other hand, he felt that what he had understood was so subtle and hard to see that he doubted whether others would be capable of finding freedom as he had done. He knew that rational thought was insufficient: you could not just think your way to enlightenment. He saw that many people were so caught up in pursuing pleasure that it would hinder them from finding the truth he had discovered. Fortunately, his compassion won out. He had a vision of a pool of lotuses with flowers at different stages of development, stretching from those as tight buds deep in the pool, through those beginning to open closer to the surface, to those fully open in the sunlight. In the same way, he saw that, although all beings had the potential for awakening, some would find it much easier to follow what he had done.

The Buddha set out at first to teach those who had taught or supported him. His former meditation teachers were dead, so instead he sought out his former disciples who had helped him in his ascetic practices. When he found his five disciples, they were at first reluctant to respond to him, yet they couldn't but be moved by his new radiance. He entered into dialogue with them and gradually one by one they came to his realization; they too became awakened.[8]

The Buddha spent the remaining 45 years of his life wandering the plains of India teaching people from all strands of society the path that could lead them to enlightenment. Many of them made real spiritual progress, bringing greater happiness and fulfilment to their lives, and some like the Buddha himself realized full awakening.

The Spread of Buddhism

During the Buddha's life, an increasing spiritual community (the *Sangha*) developed around him. The *Sangha* was comprised of people who took his example and teachings to heart and put them into practice in their own lives. After his death, the *Sangha* continued to grow as his disciples, following the Buddha's example, spread his teachings (the *Dharma*). A significant increase in the popularity of Buddhism followed the conversion to Buddhism of Ashoka, Emperor of the Mauryan Empire.[9] Gradually, Buddhism spread throughout India and most of south-east Asia.[10]

Inevitably, over time different schools of Buddhism developed emphasising different aspects of the Buddha's teaching. Broadly three main waves or developments may be discerned: early Buddhism, *Mahāyāna* and *Vajrayāna*, each appearing roughly 500 years after the other.

Early Buddhism

Early Buddhism is sometimes called the *Hīnayāna* (literally, Little Vehicle), although this is a derogatory term used by the *Mahāyāna* (literally, Great Vehicle) to distinguish itself from earlier forms of Buddhism. There were a number of different schools of early Buddhism, but the only one that has continued to the present day is *Theravādin*. This is the main form of Buddhism that is practised in Sri Lanka, Thailand, Cambodia, Myanmar and Laos. For the first few centuries following the time of the Buddha, teachings were passed down orally. Gradually, they were committed to writing. The *Theravāda* has maintained a very complete canon, in the Pāli language. The oldest strata of the Pāli canon may be the closest we can get to the actual words of the Buddha. *Theravādin* Buddhism has tended to be conservative in nature. It has emphasized monks as the main practitioners of the *Dharma*, with laypeople in a subordinate role of supporting the monks through giving alms and other requirements.

The Four Noble Truths

Many Buddhist teachings are in lists. This was to help memorize them, since in an oral tradition practising the teachings required learning them by heart. Important examples from early Buddhism include the Four Noble Truths, the Threefold Way and the Noble Eightfold Path.

The First Noble Truth is the truth of suffering. This is not to imply that life is only suffering. Instead, the Buddha was pointing out that some pain is inevitable, especially in the way that we usually live our lives. Moreover, the Buddha drew attention to suffering, because it can motivate us to change.

Craving, the cause of suffering, is the Second Noble Truth. The Buddha suggested that a lot of the pain that we experience comes from wanting what we don't have, and not wanting what we do have. It also stems from fear of losing what is dear to us, or from fear of getting what we don't want.

The Buddha declared that he had found an end to suffering, which is *nirvāna*, or awakening. This is the Third Noble Truth.

The Noble Eightfold Path is the Fourth Noble Truth. These are eight stages or aspects of the path which can lead us to awakening.[11] The eight steps are divided into three main sections (known as the Threefold Way): ethics, meditation and wisdom. Ethics or skilful actions form the foundation, which enables our meditation to flourish. As our meditation deepens we can develop wisdom, which ultimately leads to enlightenment.

Mahāyāna Buddhism

The *Mahāyāna* emphasizes the altruistic dimension of Buddhism in the form of the Bodhisattva, the spiritual hero who devotes countless lifetimes to help beings gain awakening.[12] The *Mahāyāna* originated in India, but then spread to become the main form of Buddhism in China, Tibet, Nepal, Mongolia, Vietnam, Korea and Japan. As well as accepting the earlier texts, it promoted a large corpus of

Mahāyāna sūtras. These scriptures are often richly symbolic and feature arche-typal Buddhas and Bodhisattvas. Different schools have tended to place greater importance on one or a few *Mahāyāna sūtras*. Zen is a form of *Mahāyāna* Buddhism. *Sōtō* Zen stresses sustained sitting meditation, called *zazen*. *Rinzai* Zen is associated with meditating on a *kōan*, a seemingly insoluble problem, such as, 'what is the sound of one hand clapping?'

Vajrayāna Buddhism

The *Vajrayāna* (Diamond Way or Vehicle) is a further development within *Mahāyāna* and often subsumed within it. By contrast with the *Mahāyāna* ideal of gaining awakening over many lifetimes, the *Vajrayāna* stresses the direct turn-ing towards reality and the possibility of gaining enlightenment within a single lifetime. There is a strong emphasis on ritual and the need for initiation into the *Vajrayāna* teachings (called *Tantras*) through a teacher. The *Vajrayāna* is particu-larly characteristic of Tibetan Buddhism, although it is also practised in Japan.

All three branches of Buddhism were extant in India up until the virtual disap-pearance of Buddhism there in the Middle Ages with the rise of Islam and the resurgence of Hinduism. More recently, there has been a revival of Buddhism in India following the conversion of Ambedkar, the architect of the Indian constitu-tion, to Buddhism in 1956.[13]

Western Buddhism

As Buddhism spread to new cultures it adapted to and was moulded by the cul-ture it met. This is perhaps especially true of the entry of Buddhism into China, which at that time was already a highly sophisticated culture. Although Buddhism has been known of in the West since the nineteenth century, serious practice of Buddhism really only gained momentum from the middle of the twentieth cen-tury. With the ease of modern communication and travel, most Eastern forms of Buddhism are practised in the West and, in addition, there are the beginnings of new forms and practices as Buddhism enters into dialogue with Western culture.

The Significance of the Buddha's Life for Us Today

Growing up in rural Yorkshire, although not unhappy in my home life, I found village life at times stifling and felt gnawed at by the existential quest for meaning in my life. I liked to take myself off into the surrounding woods and hills. Viewing the village from the perspective of the hills or experiencing the uplifting expanse of wide open moorland felt liberating and exhilarating. Without putting it into words at the time, I learned that I could change my mental state by dwelling in the wilderness. I had a sense of something that pointed to greater meaning, although it would be some time before I found the path that would give meaning to my life. Later reading the simple account of the Buddha's going forth, resonated strongly with my experience of the contrast between home life with its constraints and the sense of freedom of the outdoors.

For many other people, it is an encounter with one of the first three sights that is the spur to a spiritual quest. Suffering shows up in its many forms: the loss of a loved one, a serious illness, dissatisfaction with our work or the break-up of a relationship may provoke a crisis that has us looking for greater meaning in our lives. Sometimes it can be less dramatic. The more we pay attention to our wider experience, the more we see about us the inevitability of old age, sickness and death. However, living a fast urban twenty-first-century lifestyle we can seem to live in a bubble in which these things don't exist more than perhaps the occasional inconvenient cold. Travelling to work in a rush hour tube or going to the cinema in an affluent part of town, we may not see many elderly people, as though they had all been kept away from our sight. We may not come across real illness unless we happen to work in a hospital and corpses are quickly tidied away in boxes in chapels of 'rest'.

After his enlightenment, the Buddha encouraged his disciples to reflect on the following:

> *I am subject to ageing; I cannot escape ageing.*
> *I am subject to illness; I cannot escape illness.*
> *I am subject to death; I cannot escape death.*[14]

These reflections, prompted or not by what is happening around us in our life, can act as a catalyst to the bigger questions in life and can move us to engage in a spiritual search for greater meaning. They bring home both the universality of suffering and the uncomfortable fact that this will happen to me, pricking the bubble that our youth-focused culture can keep us locked in. To open us to a spiritual life we need both a degree of dissatisfaction with our current life and a sense of the possibility of something more, much as Siddhartha did in seeing the four sights. To take up spiritual practice we need the fourth sight: an example of the possibility of following the spiritual life. This might come from reading a book or hearing about Buddhism on the television or radio. However, perhaps the most compelling experience is meeting someone who is already practising Buddhism. For me, it was getting to know a fellow student who was a Buddhist. I caught his enthusiasm for the *Dharma* and, because he was a medical student like me at the time, it seemed a real possibility to follow his example and practise the *Dharma*, just as the Buddha had followed the example of the wanderer he came across before going forth on his quest.

CHAPTER 2

Starting with Mindfulness

Hard it is to train the mind,
which goes where it likes and does what it wants.
But a trained mind brings health and happiness.[1]
  —The Dhammapada, verse 35

If you go to a Buddhist centre, the first thing you are likely to be taught is meditation. Indeed, this is often the reason why people first attend a Buddhist centre. Quite likely the meditation that you will be taught is one based on mindfulness, such as the mindfulness of breathing. This is no accident, since meditation and especially mindfulness meditation are core to the Buddha's teaching. Practising mindfulness can have an immediate effect helping us to be more awake to our lives, thereby enriching them. When the Buddha gained enlightenment he is thought to have been practising something like the mindfulness of breathing. His very last words to his disciples before passing away were, 'With mindfulness, strive on'. Over the last 30 years mindfulness has been widely taken up by Western psychologists to treat a number of disorders including chronic pain, recurrent depression, anxiety and addiction.

What is Mindfulness?

The term mindfulness is used to translate a number of words found in Buddhist texts and is rich with connotations. The chief word it translates is *sati* (in Pāli; *smrti* in Sanskrit). *Sati* is related to the verb *sarati* to remember. As well as being translated as mindfulness, *sati* is often translated as awareness. So the basic meaning of mindfulness in Buddhism is awareness with the sense of remembering, recollecting or coming back to oneself and one's experience. This awareness has a warm and friendly quality. It's like the sort of attention a friend you haven't seen for some time might give you, with their curiosity to know how you are and what has been happening to you, and a friend who is happy to hear you out without rushing to jump in with their own judgements and biases about your experience. *Sati* is often linked with another word, *sampajāna*, which means clearly knowing, sometimes translated as clear comprehension of purpose. *Sampajāna* implies knowing what we are about, what our purpose is. For example, cycling and being aware of the body sensations of the legs pedalling, of the touch of the air on our face and the sights around us are all *sati*. Knowing where you are going and therefore which road to take at the traffic lights is *sampajāna*. Walking in the park and paying attention to the colour of autumn leaves is *sati*. Reflecting that you too are impermanent and that you want to make the most of this brief life is *sampajāna*.

Sometimes we recognize that we've not been very mindful. We walk into a room and can't remember what we came into the room for. Or we are returning home from work and had intended to stop off at the supermarket on the way home, but before we realize it we have passed the turning and are continuing on our normal route home. We have been running on automatic pilot. Being able to operate without too much conscious awareness is, of course, immensely helpful. First learning to drive a car, it's clunky and difficult to co-ordinate all the actions. Later we can change gear, accelerate or brake, negotiate the traffic, all while having a conversation with a passenger. Although automatic pilot is helpful for operating our lives, it also has a deadening effect. Our activities become routine and dull. We miss the detail and perhaps some of the beauty of our experience.

Mindfulness brings our attention onto what is actually happening moment by moment (*sati*) as well as keeping us in contact with our larger purpose (*sampajāna*). It is like turning up the brightness level in our lives, so that we are more in contact with the immediate freshness and richness of our experience. A tree is no longer merely a tree, but a whole intricate universe of beauty.

When the Buddha went forth, he set out to find answers to existential questions. Through awakening he found complete liberation of mind. If we too wish to follow in his footsteps and find freedom, the starting point has to be awareness of our mind. This is the work of mindfulness. We need to develop a more and more subtle awareness of ourselves, so that we are able to make choices about how we work with our minds and respond to our lives.

Breath and Body

Mindfulness can be developed towards any aspect of our experience: our thoughts, our feelings and emotions, the world around us, other people, the very nature of existence (a topic we will take up in chapter 10). However, the most efficacious foundation for mindfulness in all these areas is awareness of the breath and the body.

In mindfulness meditation we bring our attention onto the sensations of the breath or the sensations more widely in the body. If we are following the breath, we try to be as interested as we can in the sensations of breathing. We may notice the breath entering the body brushing our nostrils, we might feel it filling our chest or we could feel movement in our belly. In a technological age, in which a lot of time is given over to involvement with computers, mobile devices or television, it can be easy to lose contact with awareness of our body. Mindfulness of breath and body can act as an antidote to being too caught up in our heads and abstract realities divorced from actual sense experience.

Our minds have a tendency to roam off into anticipated futures or daydreams about the past. Body awareness brings us back into the present.

Patterns of the Mind

The basic instruction for mindfulness meditation is that we bring our awareness onto the object of the meditation, for example the breath, and whenever our mind wanders off we notice where the mind has gone to then return to the breath. In doing this we are learning three main skills. Firstly, by noting what distracts us, we begin to recognize the habitual patterns of the mind. Becoming more aware of our mental patterns we are less likely to be driven by them and have more chance of responding to them in helpful ways. Secondly, by returning to the breath we step out of the process of being caught up in whatever had taken hold of our attention. This can be a helpful way of responding to unproductive, repetitive mental patterns. Thirdly, we learn to include the breath more easily into our awareness. This can help us to stay calm, especially in moments of difficulty.

The Buddha listed five chief patterns that are minds can get caught up in: sense desire, aversion, anxiety, sleepiness and doubt. These are described below.

1. Sense Desire

One of the strongest patterns of the mind is a movement towards objects or experiences that we perceive as pleasant. This natural movement of the mind fuels our desire for food, sex, gadgets, money, fame and praise. We see this pattern writ large in corporate greed right down to the tiniest movements of our mind, such as the glance of our eyes towards someone we find attractive. I find it instructive to watch my mind on retreat.[2] At meal times, for example, propelled by barely registered attraction, I can find it telling to notice whom I end up sitting next to at the table. Even as I am eating the first serving, I might catch the thought forming in my mind about whether there will be seconds.

2. Aversion

The opposite movement to sense desire is aversion in which we push away unwanted experiences. This too can range from mild irritation at the inclement weather to outright violence and warfare. We see it in road rage and the frustration of our computer not working. Queuing is another place to spot ill-will arising. It's as though we hold a belief that the world should be organized around us so as not to inconvenience us in any way. When it doesn't go our way, aversion arises.

3. Anxiety

This can manifest in the body as restlessness. Sometimes sitting in a collective meditation it can feel as though the final bell will never come and our body becomes more and more tense and fidgety. Anxiety shows up in the mind with worries about our health, our future, and our loved ones. It can paralyse us and prevent us from living our lives more fully.

4. Sleepiness

Sometimes when we sit to meditate we find ourselves overcome with tiredness. Our thoughts start to go woolly and dreamy, it's hard to make any effort, our posture slumps and we might even completely fall asleep. If our lives are filled with rushing around, we may not notice that we are tired until we come to sit down. Without all the stimulation the tiredness appears and takes over our mind and body — a bit like someone pulling the plug out. In the space of a few minutes we can change from alertness to barely being able to keep upright. This sleepiness can also be a way of blotting out unwanted experience. If something difficult is starting to appear it can be the mind's way of checking out to avoid the difficulty. More simply, it can be that we are just not interested in our experience, as in the sleepiness that we might notice in a dull meeting at work after lunch.

5. Doubt

A more subtle pattern that can be hard to notice is doubt. This is not a matter of genuine questioning of something that we want to know the answer to. Instead, it is a way of avoiding making a decision or a commitment by throwing up a fog of spurious arguments. It can appear in meditation as lack of confidence in our own ability to meditate or thoughts that the practices don't work for us — without really giving them a proper try.

> Debbie started going to meditation classes with a friend. It had been her friend's idea, and Debbie didn't really know what to expect, but was willing to give it a try. To her surprise, she found that she felt relaxed during the meditation, which continued for some time afterwards. During one meditation, she felt a whole new level of tranquillity descend on her, the like of which she had never experienced before. Looking forward to the next time she meditated, she was disappointed to discover that she felt tense and anxious. Over the next few weeks, each time she sat to meditate she found her mind was busy with anxious thoughts about her work or her relationship. She was thinking of giving up meditation, but talking it through with one of the teachers, she was encouraged to notice if anything else was happening and she persisted.
>
> As Debbie continued to meditate she noticed a sickening feeling in her stomach associated with thoughts that she could not and would never be able to meditate. She saw too that underlying her anxiety about her work were insecurities about whether she could do the work and fears of being found out as not good enough. Similar doubts were emerging in her relationship, in which she wasn't sure if she was with the right person or whether they really cared for her.

Debbie's experience is not atypical and illustrates how the mental patterns described above can show up. Coming to meditation with few preconceptions, Debbie was able to be open, and experienced an unexpected deep calmness. This phenomenon of a deep meditation experience associated with an open-minded attitude in someone new to meditation is referred to as 'beginner's mind'. Understandably, she wanted to repeat the experience, but in doing this created a mind of wanting something, which did not allow her to relax. Moreover, she started to become aware of her habitual mind states, especially of anxiety, which she carried around a lot of the time. Underneath the anxiety was doubt, expressed as a lack of confidence in herself and her choices.

This list of five mental patterns is not exhaustive, of course, and sometimes they come in combinations. As Debbie became more aware of her tendency to doubt, she could notice that often the doubt and anxiety arose together. For myself, my mind has a default to planning, which can be a mixture of sense desire and anxiety. Sometimes there is more of the sense desire element — how can I get the goodies I hanker after. Sometimes it has a more anxious flavour — working out the best way to avoid a feared outcome.

The patterns in themselves are not necessarily a problem. Sense desire can direct us to what is supportive for our well-being, just as aversion and anxiety can be protective. Sleepiness can show us that we are tired and need a rest, and even doubt can give us a clue that there is something difficult that we need to pay attention to. However, often these patterns are unhelpful or out of proportion with the actual situation. For a while in meditation, I would keep finding myself planning what I was going to say in a job interview. Of course, some planning for an interview makes sense. In this case, however, the interview was not going to take place for another two-and-a-half years! Anxiety was clearly driving me. When we recognize a habit like this, we might want to do something about it.

Misconceptions About Meditation

When I am teaching meditation I sometimes ask people what they think meditation is about. Not infrequently people say it is about 'emptying the mind'. This is a particularly insidious and unhelpful view of meditation. Our thoughts almost never stop, so when the mind doesn't empty we think either we can't meditate or that meditation doesn't work. If we are on retreat doing a lot of meditation then sometimes we can become absorbed in, for example, the sensations of the breath and the mind becomes much quieter. Occasionally, this can happen when someone is new to meditation; a fresh openness and interest can bring a 'beginner's mind' experience. Beginner's mind can be helpful in showing the possibilities of meditation and, understood correctly, can point to the importance of coming at our meditation in a fresh way without preconceptions. Understandably, often people try to recreate the experience. Unfortunately, however, the very attempt to force it into being creates the conditions that prevent it from happening, for such forcing is the antithesis of openness and interest, invariably leading to frustration and doubt in the practice.

We live in a world with a lot of external stimulation. When we shut our eyes and sit still in meditation our mind does not just stop. Instead, we experience the effects of all that stimulation as it reverberates through the mind — images from movies we have seen, re-running of arguments from the day, recollection of plans we intend to execute — as well as all our mental patterns forged from a lifetime of habits. Our meditation is just this: coming into relationship with all of our habits again and again as our minds jumps around like a monkey swinging from tree to tree or like so many clothes rotating in a tumble dryer. If we expect our mind to empty, we'll be in for a big disappointment, which will only get in the way of engaging with and having an effective meditation practice. If we try to force our mind to be empty, pushing away the contents of our mind, we may temporarily have a sense of calm. However, rather than a full, rich sense of tranquillity, we have something thin and tense from which, sooner or later, there will be an unpleasant rebound that can completely put us off meditation. Trying to empty the mind is like putting a piece of glass on the sea to try and smooth out the waves. Practising mindfulness is like learning to ride the waves, which sometimes may be relatively calm, but more often will be rough and even stormy, and never without at least some motion.

Mindfulness Outside of Meditation

The aim of mindfulness practice is to become as fully aware of our mind at all times. Mindfulness meditation is like a laboratory. Under conditions of little external distraction, we can give more of our attention to what is happening in our body and mind. Formal meditation like this should be balanced by practices to help us become aware in the more complex situation of going about our daily lives. In principle, we can be mindful at any time, although remembering to do so is tricky. Good ways of getting into the habit of being mindful when we are not formally meditating is to bring awareness to our body or breath when we are doing a relatively simple activity such as having a shower, washing the dishes or going for a walk. When I was on-call in a large hospital, I found it helpful to practise mindfulness after I had been called to another ward. Instead of getting caught up in worrying about what I was going to meet on the ward, I would bring my attention to the soles of my feet or if I were outside between buildings I would notice the weather and savour the air on my face. I found that this led to me arriving on the ward in a much better state to deal with the situation than if I had spent the previous few minutes just worrying about it. I would be calmer and more able to be open and responsive to what was happening.

Another approach to developing mindfulness in our daily lives is what is known as the 'breathing space'. In its simplest form, we just pause and take a few mindful breaths. In the three minute or three step version of the breathing space, we first notice how we are feeling, then we bring our attention onto the breath and then we expand our awareness to include sensations in the whole of the body. The three minutes is just a guideline; it can be shortened or lengthened depending on the situation. The great thing about the breathing space exercise is that we can do it at any time. Good opportunities are waiting in line at the supermarket checkout, being stuck at traffic lights, or while having a cup of tea or sitting on the bus. One job I had involved hospital wards calling me on the bedside telephone at night. Being roused from deep sleep, to pick up a phone and respond coherently and kindly to the request for assistance down the line, I found testing. I started doing a mini breathing space in which I picked up the phone, held it arm's length for a breath or two, and then spoke to the person calling me. I found this helped me to be less irritable to the person on the other end of the line. The essence of the breathing space is putting in a little gap in our habitual reactions to our experience. This gives us a chance to regroup and catch automatic habits that unchecked might get us into trouble.

Practising Mindfulness Meditation

There are a number of versions of mindfulness meditation. Perhaps the simplest is the two-stage mindfulness of breath and body, which is described below. Another excellent way to practise mindfulness meditation is the mindfulness of breathing in four stages.[3]

Guided Meditation: Mindfulness of Breath and Body

Preparation

Before you begin to meditate try to spend a few minutes setting yourself up for meditation. You might like to light a candle or some incense. If you have time you could tidy your room a little or have a cup of tea and sit quietly.

Once you are ready, settle yourself onto your cushion or chair. Bring awareness to sensations in your body, especially the contact with the ground and the chair or cushion. Take time to notice what is going on the body and as best you can, allowing the body to settle like a sheet coming to rest on the ground.

Stage One

Gradually bring awareness onto the sensations of breathing. You might feel the rise and fall of the chest or the expansion of the belly. You could notice the sensations at just one point such as sensations as the breath enters and leaves the nostrils, or you could follow the full experience of the breath from first entering the body, right down into the belly and then all the way back out again. As best you can, try to be interested in the qualities of the breath. Is your breath long or short? Is it deep or shallow? Is it smooth or rough? You don't need to try to control the breath in any way or have any special sort of breathing; you just follow it as best you can moment by moment just as it is.

From time to time you will notice that you mind has wandered off. That's ok — it's just what minds do. Make a note of where your mind has gone to, then gently come back again to the breath. You are likely to need to do this again and again. It doesn't matter how many times the mind wanders off, each time that you notice you've gone off, you note what's taken up your mind and come back to the breath. At the point of noting your mind has gone off, you are being mindful once again.

Stage Two

Now expand your awareness to include any sensations in the body. You might notice the contact of your feet on the ground or the feel of your clothes against your skin or one part of the body resting against another or sensations deep within the body. Whatever shows up you try to attend to it with interested and kindly awareness. What exactly are the sensations like? How long do they go on for? Do they change in any way?

As before, whenever you find that your mind has wandered off, take the opportunity to notice what your mind has got caught up in and then, without getting into analysing what has happened, return to sensations of the body. If you find it helpful when your mind goes off, you can note it with a simple label such as 'anxiety' or 'planning' or 'daydreaming' or even just 'thinking'.

Concluding the Practice

Bring the practice to a close gently. Let go of trying to be aware of anything in particular, let go of any effort and just remain seated for a minute or so before ending the meditation.

CHAPTER 3

Working with Difficult Thoughts and Emotions

When the heart
is cut or cracked or broken
Do not clutch it
Let the wound lie open

Let the wind
From the good old sea blow in
To bathe the wound with salt
And let it sing

Let a stray dog lick it
Let a bird lean in the hole and sing
A simple song like a tiny bell
And let it ring.[1]

—Michael Leunig

About 18 months after I had first started meditating, I was approaching medical finals — the last exams to qualify as a doctor. Whenever I sat to meditate my mind turned to all those questions that I might be asked about in my exams. There seemed to be an impossibly large body of knowledge for me to get my head around — all the things that could go wrong with the body or the mind and how to treat them. My mind spiralled off into anxiety. In fact, meditation seemed to be making my anxiety worse and in the end I stopped meditating.

Sooner or later through mindful practice we are likely to run into uncomfortable experiences. There is no escaping that there will be times when meditation is going to be challenging. We might find old memories surfacing that have not been resolved, and we may find this disturbing. Difficult aspects of our current lives may present themselves to us more and more forcibly (like my anxiety about my exams). Or we notice that we have repetitive patterns of thoughts and emotions that appear in our mind again and again. These repetitive patterns can be annoying, disheartening or extremely painful depending on their nature. Yet despite that they are strangely sticky and hard to shake off.

Rumination and Catastrophic Thinking

There are two particular patterns of mind that cause trouble to many people: rumination and catastrophic thinking. Rumination can fill up mental space and create difficulties for a lot of us. In particular, it is one of the key mental activities that can show up in meditation in people who are prone to depression. A typical scenario is that something has happened to make you feel upset. Perhaps you receive a call from a friend cancelling an arrangement that you had made to go to the movies together or your boss at work speaks a little sharply to you when asking you about a task. You are feeling a bit upset and your mind starts to analyse why this is. What did you do to make your boss so brusque with you? Why has your friend cancelled? Is it that they don't like you anymore? Have you done something to offend them or your boss?

Rumination is like a dog worrying a bone. You go over and over in your mind what has happened. This has the effect of making you feel more upset and depressed. In turn, this stimulates more rumination, triggering a downward spiral into deeper depression.

With rumination we are trying to sort out a problem, but, paradoxically, it has the effect of making matters worse. It feels like we are doing something about the problem by analysing and going over what happened again and again, which may be one of the reasons rumination can be so hard to let go of. Current approaches to cognitive-behavioural therapy (CBT), including Mindfulness-Based Cognitive Therapy (MBCT), target rumination owing to its central role in maintaining recurrent depression.

Catastrophic thinking is another sticky thought form that can take over our minds. This is what was happening to me as I approached finals. Perhaps in a crowded supermarket we start to feel hot and uncomfortable. The heart races a little faster and the thought 'Am I having a heart attack?' pops into the mind causing a surge of anxiety. Taking the thought at face value can lead to a spiral of anxiety or a panic attack as we become more convinced that we really are having a heart attack. 'Did I remember to lock the door?' shows up in our thoughts just after we have left home. A creeping suspicion that we have left the door open gains ground and more thoughts appear about someone breaking in and stealing our valuable possessions, and with this a sense of anxiety grows.

Of course, it could be correct that we *have* forgotten to lock the door. We go back and find that is in fact locked. We set off again, but again the thought and the doubt appears in the mind as to whether we have really locked the door, and with that comes mounting anxiety, even though at some level we know that we have just checked the door. These sorts of obsessive-compulsive thoughts and anxiety can cause passing discomfort or form deeply entrenched habits that can be disabling with repeated cycles of anxiety and behaviours (in this case checking) to alleviate the anxiety.

Turning Towards Our Experience

When difficulties arise in our meditation, whether repeated thoughts, unpleasant emotions or painful physical sensations, we need to change strategy from just noting the experience and returning to the object of the meditation such as the breath. What is required is what can often amount to a 180-degree shift from what we want to do and, indeed, often what we habitually do. Our default position is typically to try and push away the uncomfortable experience. That's an understandable reaction. It is unpleasant and, of course, we would much rather it cleared off and would like to send it on its way. The trouble is this strategy simply doesn't work.

It may be possible to avoid some external things, such as places or people we don't like. Even then, however, we are not likely to always be able to escape these situations. Most of us at some time may have had to work with someone we don't like and that we can't avoid, or be somewhere we would rather not be, such as the dentist's. With internal experiences we can try to distract ourselves from what is happening and this may work temporarily, but sooner or later it will return. Usually, trying to push the experience away makes it worse. For example, we notice a painful sensation in our leg. In trying to push it away we end up tensing up. As in the poem, we clutch our wound. This only makes the pain worse. Our efforts to keep out unpleasant experiences not only make them worse but also can use up a lot of energy in trying to keep them at bay.

Ivan had been practising meditation on and off for a few years before he had a motorbike accident. He was badly hurt, and although he had made a good recovery he was left with constant pain in his back. The painkillers helped, but not completely. His doctors had said that he needed to learn to live with the pain and had told him not to lift any heavy weights. Ivan didn't see how he could live with the pain and the prospect of not being able to pick up his two-year-old son seemed even worse than the back pain itself. In desperation, Ivan decided to resume meditating. However, whereas in the past he had often found meditation relaxing, now he found that he could not get comfortable because of the back pain and his mind was in turmoil.

The meditation teacher encouraged Ivan to turn towards and explore the painful physical and mental sensations. Ivan initially found this a real struggle, but gradually he began to be able to sit with what was happening. He used the breath as a gentle probe to explore the sensations in his back, breathing into the sensations. As he paid more careful attention, he found that the seemingly solid and constant pain broke up into a procession of changing sensations. At times they were sharp and intense, and then they could be duller and vaguer. They seemed to move about different parts of his back. As he explored further, he sometimes noticed tightness in his chest. These sensations seemed to be associated with thoughts and feelings of being a bad father, blaming himself for being careless in having the accident, or anger at his predicament. Slowly he learned to step back from the thoughts and feelings and stay with the sensations in his chest, allowing them to be there. As he did that, the feelings became less overpowering. The pain in his back did not go away completely but as he learned to accept the painful thoughts, not getting so caught up in them, and to follow the changing sensations in his back, he found that he was less distressed and was managing to live more easily with the back pain.

Ways to Help Us Turn Towards Our Experience

1. Accept, Don't Reject

Our first task when difficulties arise is to acknowledge that difficulties have arisen. We accept the fact of their reality, simply because that is what is happening. There is a kind of wisdom here, because we are facing up to how things are rather than trying to convince ourselves of a fabrication.

By *acceptance* I don't mean resignation. This is not a passive, 'might as well run me over', giving in and giving up. It's more like standing up to what is actually going on. Neither does it mean that we like or approve of what is there. Real acceptance has a quality of friendliness and curiosity towards what is happening. It's possible to be friendly without liking or approving. Ivan would certainly have much preferred not to have had the accident and the pain that followed. What made a real difference for Ivan was stopping berating himself for what had happened and being willing to be fully present with the thoughts, feelings and physical sensations in a moment by moment way.

When I'm teaching this approach people sometimes ask me what is the difference between acceptance and rumination. They fear that if they turn towards it or accept it they will just end up wallowing in it or making it worse. It's a fine line to tread and needs some practice to get the hang of it. Body awareness, as described below, can help to give us a different place from which to view our thoughts so that in accepting them we don't stay stuck in them. First, we need to acknowledge what is present in our mind. When rumination arises we need to recognize, 'this is rumination'. We don't berate ourselves for the fact — after all, from the ordinary mind's point of view, it's understandable that this is what the thinking mind is doing. The same principle applies to catastrophic thinking; we recognize and accept what is taking place, acknowledging 'Okay, here I go again, getting caught up in catastrophic thoughts'.

2. Move Towards and Investigate

With an attitude of friendliness and curiosity we start to explore what is going on. However, rather than explore the thoughts directly, which is likely to get us caught back up in them, our primary focus is the body. How does this feel in the body right now? Where exactly in the body can we feel the anxiety? Emotions always have a bodily aspect to them. With anxiety, we might find tensing in the shoulders or butterflies in the stomach. With depression, we might notice a pain in the chest or tightness in the throat. With every set of repeated thoughts, even when there doesn't appear to be much emotion, there will be some bodily sensations running along with them. Sometimes they can be subtle and — especially if we are not used to paying attention to our body — hard to discern. It might be just a slight clenching of the jaw or tightening in the hands.

Having located the body sensations associated with our thoughts or emotions, we start to investigate them. We don't need to worry about whether these particular sensations are actually associated with this set of thoughts; we just pay attention to whatever sensations are happening at the same time as the thoughts. The breath is very helpful to use as an anchor and a sort of probe with which to explore the body sensations. We can breathe into the sensations, 'letting the sea wind blow in'. Even if it is a part of the body that the breath does not physically go into, such as the thighs, we can still have a sense of directing the breath towards what is going on. As best we can, we are curious about the sensations. Are they dull or sharp? Are they absolutely static or do they change? Do they have a shape or colour?

We stay with the sensations until they have changed. Generally, if we get out of the way by not adding to what is going on with more thoughts and fears, the sensations will move on. It is sometimes said that feelings want to be felt. Feelings and emotions are kept in place by avoiding them or feeding them, especially with our judging thoughts about them. What we mean by feeling our feelings is staying with the body sensations so that they can run their course.

If the sensations are particularly intense, we can breathe on the edge of the part of the body where there are the uncomfortable sensations. Perhaps we have a sense of something unpleasant that we really don't want to go anywhere near. So instead of plunging in to the centre of the area with the difficult sensations, we direct our attention, using the breath, to the periphery. Our experience can be layered, rather like an onion — for example, we might experience anger about feeling depressed, and this is covered by feeling anxious about being angry. As we gently approach the sensations associated with the anxiety, they may begin to change and reveal the anger or depression underneath. If it's too difficult to keep with the sensations until they have changed, we can dip in and out. We move onto the sensations, or the edge of the cloud of sensations, for a while, then return back to just being with the breath or other body sensations that don't feel so threatening. We can alternate between steadying the mind on the breath and turning towards the difficulties. In time, we will get better at holding more and more difficult experience. Mindful practice here is like developing muscles in the gym; it allows us to more easily contain whatever our mind throws at us.

A couple of years after my medical finals, I was preparing for my first set of psychiatric examinations. I noticed the same thing happening: my mind heading off into a vortex of fear with thoughts about all the things I might be asked but didn't know the answers to. This time something different happened. My mindfulness practice was stronger and I was able to accept that my body and mind were filling up with anxiety. Yes, it was unpleasant, and yes, I didn't want it, but here it was anyway. I was more able this time to just stay with those unpleasant sensations: the churning in the belly, the heat in the hands, the tension in the shoulders and tightness in the mind. I could find some space around it all and let it be there. It waxed and waned, but it never got out of control and this time my meditation was a support that kept me going through the difficult time.

3. Look for the Deeper Meaning

Another approach that can complement the practices of acceptance and turning towards is to look for the deeper meaning of our troubles. We get anxious or angry (or any other emotion) for a reason. We have been running these habits for a long time — even when they are uncomfortable and unhelpful — because that's the best way our mind has come up with to deal with particular situations. Often the function of such automatic responses is to protect our sense of comfort or our self-image. Anger lashes out to protect us when we are feeling hurt. Anxiety fills our mind to get us to act or avoid some disastrous anticipated catastrophe. Rumination takes over the mind to attempt to solve a pressing problem such as why we are feeling depressed right now.

However, it doesn't work just to know in an abstract way that our anger is protecting us from feeling hurt and then tell the mind to stop it, like a teacher standing at the front of the class wagging their finger at the distressed child and pointing to the answer on the blackboard. We need to get down alongside the angry mind and understand from its point of view what it is trying to do. This requires some patience and sympathy towards the difficult emotions. We take an interest in the mind and enquire what it's trying to do, but it's a question of finding the right voice. One time when I was particularly gripped with planning in meditation, I found a way of saying to myself, 'Paramabandhu, you really love to plan!'. It wasn't accusatory in any way, nor sarcastic or even teasing. It was just a friendly, interested observation. In that moment, the planning fell away, and for a while I could see the futility of trying to control the universe, and let go of the attempt to control, which was driving the planning.

Once we have been able to feel into and touch the deeper meaning, we have a chance of releasing the unhelpful emotion. It's just our mind trying to protect us or sort out a problem. We can feel sympathy with the intention without having to go along with the solution the habitual mind has come up with. If we don't feel sympathy the rest of our mind will ignore our attempt to let go of the difficult emotion, and then it's business as usual. This is why kindness is so important as an aspect of mindfulness — and something we'll be taking up more fully in the next chapter. We need to approach our difficult emotions and habitual thoughts with a freshness and friendliness, like being paid attention from someone who really cares about us. It is like catching our habitual minds off guard and penetrating to the secret meaning and hurt that will only be revealed if we can put our mind at ease.

Guided Meditation: Mindfulness of Breath and Body Working with Difficult Thoughts and Emotions

Preparation

Spend some time settling into your body. Allow your awareness to descend into your body. Bring attention to the contact with the ground and the chair or cushion. Allow the body to be upright, but without straining. Easing any tension in the shoulders and allowing the hands to be supported by your lap, take time to notice what is going on in your mind. How are you feeling right now? Are you happy, sad, bored, contented, irritated or what? If you can't feel anything in particular, that's ok, just notice that. Are there any particular thoughts that are preoccupying you?

Stage One

Gradually bring awareness onto the sensations of breathing. You might feel the rise and fall of the chest or the expansion of the belly. You could notice the sensations at just one point such as sensations as the breath enters and leaves the nostrils or you could follow the full experience of the breath from first entering the body, right down into the belly and then all the way back out again. As best you can, try to be interested in the qualities of the breath. Is your breath long or short? Is it deep or shallow? Is it smooth or rough? You don't need to try to control the breath in any way or have any special sort of breathing: you just follow it as best you can moment by moment just as it is.

From time to time, you will notice that you mind has wandered off. To begin with just make a note of where your mind has gone to, then gently come back again to the breath. If you find that you are facing some difficulty in your experience — persistent or intense feelings of anxiety, distress, anger or some other emotion, or if you are caught up in recurrent, troublesome thoughts, then choose to turn towards your experience. Greet what is going on with as much friendliness and curiosity as you can muster. Use your breath to help you stay with the experience by breathing into the experience, especially the body sensations associated with what is going on. Notice just what the sensations are like and how they change moment by moment. Then, when you have spent some time doing that or the experience has changed significantly, return back to just following the breath going in and out of the body.

Stage Two

Now expand your awareness to include any sensations in the body. You might notice the contact of your feet on the ground or the feel of your clothes against your skin or one part of the body resting against another or sensations deep within the body. Whatever shows up try to attend to it with interested and kindly awareness. What exactly are the sensations like? How long do they go on for? Do they change in any way?

Then, if you find yourself caught up in a difficulty, acknowledge that your mind has been hooked into something difficult and choose to turn towards it, leaning into it. Breathe into the experience, or if it's very intense, just breathe on the edge of it, allowing your attention to float there. Be curious about the sensations underlying the thoughts and emotions, noticing where in the body they are strongest and what they are like. If you find it helpful, say to yourself: 'It's ok, whatever it is, it is already here, let me feel it'. Then, when you have spent some time with the experience or it has changed significantly, return your attention back to general body sensations.

Concluding the Practice

Bring the practice to a close gently. Let go of trying to be aware of anything in particular. Let go of any effort and just remain seated for a minute or so before ending the meditation.

CHAPTER 4

Introducing Kindness

Whatever living beings there be:
feeble or strong, tall, stout or medium,
short, small or large, without exception;
seen or unseen, those dwelling far or near,
those who are born or those who are to be born,
may all beings be happy![1]

—The Mettā Sutta

Shirley had been practising mindfulness meditation for a couple of months. She had been very keen to engage in this practice. She had read that it could help her with her tendency to depression and she had always been half on the lookout for something that could give a greater meaning to her life. Intuitively she felt meditation might point the way. Work in a corporate environment was stressful. Shirley worked long hours and still there was not enough time to complete the deadlines to her satisfaction. She easily felt criticized by her boss and was critical of herself for not working hard enough. Despite the long hours, she made time for mindfulness meditation, getting up half an hour earlier each day.

Even though she was keen to do the meditation, she was surprised at how hard it was to stay with the breath. Her mind ran off on repeatedly onto worries about work and she was beginning to feel that she was just not very good at meditation. The meditation teacher gently reminded her that the point was to notice where her mind went so that she could get to know her mind more fully. In addition, her teacher wondered to Shirley if she might be being rather critical of herself and suggested she might like to try to notice when judging appeared in her mind. With renewed vigour, Shirley took up noticing the patterns of her mind and discovered with increasing horror just how critical she was — not just of herself, but also those around her, such as her work colleagues. The extent of her fault-finding mind felt overwhelming and it seemed to her that meditation was just making things worse. She was considering giving up meditation altogether, but then instead decided to sign up for a follow-up course that was based on kindness meditation.

Why Kindness is Important

Mindfulness is only one half of the equation in terms of the fundamental qualities that we develop on the Buddhist path. The other half is kindness. We start by becoming more aware through the practice of mindfulness. However, importantly, the sort of awareness we are seeking to cultivate is a kindly one, an awareness that is imbued with friendliness and curiosity. All too easily that aspect of mindfulness gets lost or is absent as we push ahead with the practice. The meditation can develop a forced quality to it so that our sitting practice feels dry. We may find we get headaches in meditation or feel a little spaced out. Difficult emotions feel overwhelming — as Shirley discovered when she found out the extent of her critical thoughts — or, without realising it, we push them away leading to a sense of numbness or emptiness in our meditation.

Kindness is the antidote to these difficulties. An attitude of kindness may be key to successful outcome when mindfulness meditation is used for example to help depression (Mindfulness-Based Cognitive Therapy, MBCT).[2] When practising mindfulness, some people grasp quite quickly that real mindfulness has a kindly aspect to it. For others, it is a longer journey. Our lack of kindness shows up especially in our relationship to ourselves and to other people. If we just do mindfulness meditation practices the relative dearth of kindness may remain concealed from our awareness, yet at the same time it will block or slow down the effectiveness of our practice. Like Shirley, we may come to a point where our meditation seems to be making matters worse. Alternatively, we may continue for years, out of touch with our real emotions, with a sense of feeling blocked or alienated. For these reasons, practice that focuses directly on cultivating kindness is essential. Kindness meditation practices, like the *mettā bhāvanā* practice described below, centre on our relationship with ourselves and with specific others, since this is the most fruitful ground on which to bring kindness to bear.

Kindness: True and False

Some of us are allergic to the notion of developing kindness. It has an all-too-soft connotation. The mention of kindness and our worst fears of Buddhism are confirmed: it is all about complacently navel-gazing with a fuzzy warm glow and in our day-to-day life being saccharine nice or a doormat.

In his book *The Art of Being Kind,* Stefan Einhorn helpfully distinguishes between true and false kindness.[3] By false kindness, Einhorn means kindness — or rather something that appears to be kindness — that is weak, stupid or manipulative. The 'near enemy' is the term that Buddhism uses for emotions that on the surface look like the emotion in question, but are not the real thing.

Weak Kindness

Weak kindness is the doormat phenomenon. In the name of kindness we allow others to walk over us or do not challenge other people because we do not want to upset them (although more likely underneath we are fearful of getting into conflict or being criticized ourselves). So we watch a colleague at work act harshly towards someone without taking it up or we allow our partner to put us down and we just swallow it.

Stupid Kindness

'He meant well' can often be the giveaway sign of 'stupid kindness'. Although good intentions are important, they are not enough if there is not some thought and sensitivity to the likely outcome of our actions. A generalized wash of goodwill that does not see or respond to the particularities of the person we are attempting to be kind to, is not kindness.

Manipulative Kindness

Sometimes when someone gives us a present or acts in our favour we can feel coerced by it. After the event we discover there were strings attached. When someone acts with true kindness, both the person being kind and the recipient of the kindness are likely to benefit. Our awareness that we may benefit from a kind act should not stop us from trying to be kind. If we wait until our motives are completely pure, we should probably never act with kindness, and any generous-hearted impulses would wither before they are carried out. Similarly, we need not block someone's attempt to be kind to us due to our individualistic urge to be independent and not beholden to others. Manipulative kindness is where the ulterior motive is the driving force and the kind façade has a sham quality to it.

Sentimental Attachment

To these three imposters the Buddhist tradition adds another near enemy: sentimental attachment. When we fall in love with someone or watch a documentary about dolphins, the rush of warm feelings may be as much about ourselves as it is about the other person or the animal. When we fall in love and it is reciprocated, it is of course delightful. However, if you have the experience of someone falling in love with you when you don't feel the same way, you can feel uncomfortable. There are strong feelings coming your way, but they seem to be directed at an idea of you that is mostly in the other person's mind. You may be left feeling that the other person is not really seeing *you*, for who you are.

True Kindness

By contrast, true kindness has an element of wisdom to it. True kindness sees the other person more fully and reads the situation. Acting with kindness may mean having courage to stand up for other people or for ourselves, rather than being taken advantage of. Real kindness is primarily directed at benefitting its object, even though, secondarily, benefits may rebound back to us. Human as we are, we are all likely to err towards one or more of the false varieties from time to time. Being aware of them can help us to shape our impulses and emotions towards true kindness. Having clarity on what we mean by real kindness can help us to overcome any aversion or allergy towards the idea and practice of it.

Cultivating Kindness in Five Stages — the *Mettā Bhāvanā*

The main meditation practice to cultivate kindness is called the *mettā bhāvanā*. *Mettā* is a Pāli word often translated as loving kindness. *Bhāvanā* means cultivation or development, or simply meditation. Pāli is an ancient Indian language, probably fairly close to the language spoken by the Buddha. The Pāli scriptures are the most extensive and well-preserved scriptures that have come down to us from the early oral tradition.

The *mettā bhāvanā* is practised in five stages: self, a friend, a neutral person, a difficult person, and all beings. We start with ourselves. Then we move on to other people. When we bring to mind another person it is likely to be pleasurable, painful, or neither painful nor pleasurable. The next three stages cover in specific people these three principal feeling tone responses we have to people in general.[4] Broadly speaking, we like someone, we don't like someone, or we don't care. This gives us an opportunity to work with attachment, ill-will, and boredom or indifference respectively. In the final stage, having explored and worked with the range of feeling tone responses we have to specific people, we expand out to include all beings.

(1) Self

The *mettā bhāvanā* practice starts at home, with oneself. True kindness includes both ourselves and other people, and would be one-sided without both. Often people struggle with this stage. As soon as we focus on ourselves we may become aware of a host of negative criticisms or low self-esteem. A starting point, outside of this self-criticism, can be to remember how we look after ourselves even in small ways such as feeding and clothing ourselves. The very fact that we are reading this book or attempting to practise the *mettā bhāvanā* is a sign that we wish to help ourselves. In this stage it is best to try not to push too hard. It is enough to become aware of how we are actually feeling, and then with whatever is happening to gently wish ourselves well. For a long time the first stage of my own *mettā bhāvanā* practice consisted of just finding out how I felt, allowing myself to be with that and getting to know myself on that level.

(2) A Friend

In the second stage we pick a friend. The usual recommendations are to pick — at least to begin with — someone who is alive, roughly the same age and who we are not sexually attracted to. The reason for this is that when we are learning the practice we want to make it as easy as possible for us. If we choose a relatively uncomplicated friendship we won't so easily get caught up in the near enemies of *mettā*. We can bring the friend to mind — usually an enjoyable thing to do — and wish them well. We could do this, for example, by wishing them to be happy, to be free from suffering, and to have a satisfying and fulfilling life.

(3) A Neutral Person

This stage demands a greater use of our imagination. We aim to pick a person we don't have strong feelings for one way or the other. Most likely, there will be at least a little liking or disliking of the person, since within seconds of meeting someone we make some kind of appraisal of them, which will affect how we feel about them. It could perhaps be someone we see around regularly, but don't have that much to do with, like a colleague in a different department or the shopkeeper we buy our milk from. It should, nevertheless, be a real person that we have had at least a little contact with. We bring them to mind and try to get a sense of them in their world. And we wish them well too.

(4) A Difficult Person

In cultivating kindness our aim is to go beyond our likes and dislikes and develop goodwill to all beings. Hence, in the excerpt from the *Mettā Sutta* (quoted at the start of the chapter) the Buddha exhorts us to wish happiness to all beings whatsoever. This doesn't mean that we therefore have to start liking everyone or that we approve of people's actions we see as unhelpful. Rather, we recognize that this person is another human being. Like us, this person wants to be happy and doesn't want to suffer. And, in all probability, in their own way they are doing the best to be happy. This stage can be challenging, but potentially also offers rich fruits of self-discovery and transformation. Often, we don't like people because it reminds us of something we don't like in ourselves and our buttons are pushed.

Sometimes people say there is no-one they dislike. Most likely this means that we may need to look a bit deeper. The family is a good place to start! It is hard to be in relationship with someone over a long period of time without at least sometimes being irritated by them. Foibles that in a good mood can seem charming, on another day can be irksome. Nevertheless, we need to be patient. The work of the heart is usually gradual and slow. If there is someone in your life who evokes strong feelings of ill-will, it is better to wait until you are experienced and have some skill in the practice, and are in a good state. Otherwise, as I often say to people I teach, you are in danger of ending up doing the hate *bhāvanā*! However, with time, we can eventually transform how we feel towards even the most difficult person.[5]

(5) All Beings

We begin the final stage by bringing to mind all four people — oneself, the friend, the neutral person and the difficult person — with the aim of extending kindness to all four people equally. We are endeavouring to cultivate a heart that responds with kindness to all that we meet, whether ourselves or other people, whether we like or don't like them. We are relating to all four people as human beings like ourselves.

From there we extend our goodwill further. If we are meditating with others we can include everyone in the room, then everyone in the building, and then everyone in the neighbourhood. We can keep expanding as far as our imagination will take us. We might do this geographically or bring to mind different categories of people, such as all people in hospital or all people who are hungry or all people having a birthday that day. Our aim is to having a sense of goodwill that ultimately reaches out to all beings. This can include all life, not just human beings.

Some Tips for Cultivating Kindness

Kindness is Not Toothpaste!

The temptation in kindness meditation is to be overly forceful. We tend to push or try to squeeze out kindness to people like toothpaste from a tube. Needless to say, the heart does not work like this. A helpful acronym is DROPS: don't resist or push, soften. When difficult feelings or emotions arise, rather than resist them, we can try to be open and accepting of them. We allow them to be there without fighting. Instead of pushing through something, we can soften into it. If we feel blocked and there is not much happening we can soften towards that too. If critical judgments arise about how we are doing or should be doing, again we can notice and soften around those critical thoughts.

Start with Receptivity

A good place to start the practice is by tuning in with ourselves and noting how we are feeling. We get a sense of what we are bringing to the meditation that we will be working with. If we start to feel overwhelmed or stuck in the practice, it is a good idea to stop and come back to ourselves. We patiently wait for the feelings to move or for more clarity to arise. At the end of each stage we can come back to ourselves. We can check in with ourselves, grounding, before moving on to the next person.

In particular, it is worth paying attention to the sensations in the heart area, that is, in the centre of the chest. The work we are engaging in can be subtle. We might notice a small warm glow, a tenderness or a slight tremulousness. We can pay attention to these sensations without grasping after them or straining. Sometimes it can be helpful just to become aware of how we feel towards the different people in each stage and sit with that, as a short *mettā bhāvanā*, especially if we are feeling cut off from our emotions.

Intention is More Important Than Feeling

The chief aim of kindness meditation is to cultivate an intention of wishing people well. Sometimes this may result in strong warm and joyful feelings. However, this outcome is not essential. We don't need to feel discouraged then if we are not having strong emotional experiences in the meditation. In fact, the real test is what happens outside of meditation.

After Shirley had found herself struggling with mindfulness practice, she felt some trepidation at starting the new course with kindness meditation. She found the *mettā bhāvanā* hard, especially the first stage, but nevertheless she persisted. Nothing much seemed to be happening in the meditation, but then one day after a few weeks of practising she noticed that something was different in work. She found that she was getting on better with her colleagues; and the boss, who had featured regularly in her fourth stage, seemed less critical of her. She could see that her boss too was stressed and anxious. She didn't take her boss's comments to heart so much and she found that she was better able to co-operate with her and the quality of her working life seemed to change for the better.

Kindness Breathing Space

In order to help translate what we are doing on the meditation cushion to the rest of our life we can introduce an element of kindness into the breathing space. As described in chapter 2, we begin by checking in with ourselves. We notice just how we are feeling, right now, whatever that feeling is. We notice prominent thoughts, body sensations or emotions. Having gained some sense of how we are, we then bring our attention onto the breathing. As we do this, we can have a sense of breathing with kindness. In particular, breathing kindness into whatever is happening within us at this moment. We don't need to try to change anything; we just feel it and bring, as best we can, kindness to it with the breath. Finally, we extend our awareness to include the whole body, and with that can have a sense of extending kindness to all around us.

As with the breathing space described earlier, this can be done at any time. It can be longer or shorter depending on the circumstances. When we notice we feel upset or stressed, such as being stuck in a traffic jam or finding ourselves in conflict with someone, is a good time to use it. We can also use it at a regular time, to get into the habit of bringing kindness to ourselves and our world — for example, when we are on public transport or before surfing the internet after we have turned the computer on.

Practising Kindness Meditation

There are many different approaches to practising kindness meditation and we can give free rein to our imagination in how we go about it. In the practice of the *mettā bhāvanā* described below, we will be using the breath and phrases to help cultivate feelings of kindness. We can use the breath, as in the breathing space above, to breathe kindness towards our experience of ourselves and towards other people. We can use phrases to express a wish or an intention, such as 'may I be happy', or 'may this person be free from suffering'. When you use phrases (and you can use whatever phrase you resonate most strongly with), say them gently and deliberately in your mind and then pause to allow them to have an effect before repeating a phrase.

Guided Kindness Meditation

Take some time to settle into your body . . . feeling the ground beneath your feet . . . noticing the contact of the chair or cushion and allowing the chair or cushion to take your weight . . . allowing a sense of the body to be upright, but without straining . . . letting your hands settle on your lap.

Now bringing attention to your chest . . . feeling the movement of the breath in and out of the body . . . noticing sensations in the centre of the chest, in the heart area . . . noticing how you are feeling right now.

(1) Self

Bringing a sense of kindness to whatever is happening right now . . . using the breath to touch you with kindness . . . breathing in, breathing in kindness . . . if you wish, imagining the breath filling your body with kindness like beautiful white or golden light suffusing your body . . . dropping in a phrase, saying to yourself gently 'may I be well' . . . allowing the phrase to echo in your heart and noticing whatever arises . . . saying to yourself 'may I be happy' and allowing it to affect you . . . 'may I make progress' . . . not forcing or pushing, just as best you can being with whatever arises with kindness.

(2) Friend

Now bringing to mind a friend . . . noticing the effect of bringing that person to mind . . . breathing with kindness. And as you breathe out, breathing out kindness towards the friend . . . allowing your friend to fill with kindness, with golden or white light, with well-being and contentment . . . saying to yourself 'may this person be happy' . . . pausing and allowing this phrase to have an effect . . . 'may this person be at peace' . . . noticing the sensations in your chest, in the heart area, and allowing whatever arises to be there.

(3) Neutral Person

Letting go of the friend and coming back to yourself . . . still breathing with kindness . . . now bringing to mind a neutral person . . . noticing the effect of bringing this person to mind . . . breathing with kindness towards this person or imagining them breathing with kindness . . . imagining them filling with kindness, with well-being and contentment . . . dropping in a phrase 'may this person be happy'. . . . noticing the effect of the phrase . . . 'may this person be well' . . . allowing whatever arises, however slight or strong, to be there . . . touching it with the breath, with kindness.

(4) Difficult Person

Letting go of the neutral person and coming back to yourself . . . tuning into yourself again and breathing with kindness . . . now bringing to mind a difficult person . . . noticing the effect of bringing this person to mind . . . breathing out with kindness towards the difficult person and breathing in with kindness towards yourself . . . allowing the difficult person to fill with kindness, well-being and contentment . . . saying to yourself, 'may this person be happy' . . . noticing the effect of the phrase . . . 'may this person be free from suffering' . . . feeling the sensations in the heart area . . . noticing any tightening in the body; feeling into it and allowing it to soften.

(5) All Beings

Now letting go of the difficult person and coming back to yourself . . . feeling the contact with the ground and the support of the cushion or chair . . . now bringing to mind all four people: yourself, the friend, the neutral person and the difficult person. Breathing with kindness towards all four people . . . imagining all four people suffused with light of kindness, well-being and contentment . . . saying to yourself 'may we all be happy' . . . allowing the phrase to affect you . . . 'may we all be at ease' . . .

. . . gradually radiating out a sense of kindness and well-wishing, breathing with kindness . . . including all the people in the building. 'may we all be happy' . . . including all people in your immediate neighbourhood . . . 'may we all be free from suffering' . . . extending out to more and more people as far as your imagination will take you . . . 'may all beings be happy in their heart of hearts' . . . .

. . . once again coming back to yourself . . . letting go of any effort . . . sitting quietly, breathing, and gradually bringing the practice to a close.

CHAPTER 5

Living Skilfully

Experiences are preceded by mind, led by mind, and produced by mind.
If one speaks or acts with an impure mind, suffering follows even as
the cartwheel follows the hoof of the ox (drawing the cart). . . .
If one speaks or acts with a pure mind, happiness follows like a shadow
that never departs.[1]

—Dhammapada, verses 1–2

When I watch my mind in meditation, I frequently notice how it lapses into wanting pleasure — the little coffee and cake treat that I 'deserve' after some work, or coming up with rationalizations in my mind as to why I need the latest gizmo. It's quite natural. As humans we want pleasure and we want to be happy. However, we easily conflate the two. We can believe that if we seek out pleasure we will find happiness. And that is true — but only up to a point.

Studies looking at what makes us happy suggest that pleasure increases our happiness a little. Seligman, a leading researcher in this area, suggests that by sampling pleasures in a deliberate and careful way we can maximize the happiness obtained.[2] This is basic mindfulness. If we savour our food mindfully as we eat it rather than gulping it down while reading the paper with the TV on in the background, we are more likely to enjoy our food and obtain more pleasure from it. However, such pleasure gives but fleeting happiness.

A greater sense of satisfaction and happiness, according to Seligman's work, is derived from exercising our strengths and acting on our virtues. By 'strengths' Seligman means the sort of activities that we are good at or have a natural inclination for. So if we like to organize, planning and sorting out some event is likely to bring us satisfaction and a deeper happiness than mere sensory pleasure. If we like to help others, then some kind of work that benefits others is likely to increase our happiness. Virtues refers to the personal qualities that we find inspiring and believe in such as honesty or kindness.

Karma and Happiness

The Buddha spoke of karma to describe how we cause ourselves happiness or — often unwittingly — unhappiness. Karma is the relationship between our actions and the fruits of those actions, called *karma-vipāka*. Actions in Buddhism refer to body, speech and mind. What we do with our limbs, what we say with our voice, and our thoughts and emotions are all considered to be actions. Actions always have consequences. In particular, our actions will affect our own mind, in addition to any effects they have on the people and world around us.

The Buddha (and, following him, Eastern Buddhist traditions) accepted the idea of rebirth, that is, a continuation from one life to another, rather than complete annihilation at death. Karma describes how what we do in this life may affect subsequent lives. However, the Buddha made it clear that karma also describes the effects of our actions within this life.[3] Moreover, although actions will have a karmic result, not everything that happens to us is the result of karma.[4] For example, we may be feeling unhappy as the result of speaking harshly to someone (an effect of karma), or our unhappiness could be due to the biochemistry of some medication we are taking, such as steroids (an effect not a result of karma).

Critical to the effect of our actions, as described by karma, is the mind state that they are rooted in. When we act out of a mental state of kindness, clarity and contentment — a skilful mental state — it will have a beneficial effect on our own mind and our world around us. When we act with an unskilful mental state such as ill-will, craving, ignorance or lack of clarity, it will have an adverse effect. For example, if we hit somebody in anger, speak harshly to them with irritation or just feel ill-will towards someone without acting externally on our ire, it will have an unpleasant, contracting effect on our mind, aside from any adverse effect on others. Even if we don't act directly with our body or speech, the anger will affect our mind and is likely to impact on others who may pick up our vibe. Conversely, if we act with kindness, such as going out of our way to help someone, or if we speak in a kindly manner to someone, or if we hold someone in mind with kind thoughts, it will have a beneficial effect on ourselves, leading to happiness. It is also likely to benefit others.

Rather than speak in terms of good and evil, the Buddha described actions as being skilful or unskilful. Recognizing the effects of our actions and applying ourselves to benefit ourselves and others is a skill. We don't cause ourselves and others harm because we are bad, but rather because we are ignorant in the sense of not understanding clearly the effects of our actions. The practice of ethics in Buddhism, then, is to recognize the mental states that are driving our actions, to take responsibility for them, and to move towards more and more skilful actions.

Mindfulness meditation helps us to become aware of the mental states behind our actions. Each time our mind drifts off the object of meditation, such as the breath, we have an opportunity to see the direction of our mental habits. We can notice whether our mind is heading off in a skilful or an unskilful direction. Our job is then to own our mental states. If we are feeling irritable we face up to that fact, without blame towards ourselves or any trigger for our irritability. We notice with kindness the effect on our mind and, as far as we are able, the effect on others. The *mettā bhāvanā* can help us cultivate this friendly attitude towards whatever is going on in our mind. In addition, as we move through each stage of the practice we have a chance to see our mental responses to the different people in the practice. This is why it is helpful at the beginning of each stage to spend some time noticing our initial response to each person (including ourselves).

Having acknowledged and owned our mental states the next step is to guide them in a more skilful direction. We can try to ameliorate unskilful mental states and cultivate or augment skilful ones. Some of this work goes on in meditation, but the real work is putting this into practice as we go about our daily lives. This means, as far as possible, being aware of our mental states, and working with them. It also means changing our speech and behaviour. We aim to live our lives as skilfully as possible. Meditation and skilful living mutually reinforce each other.

The Five Precepts

To help us act skilfully in our lives Buddhism has produced various lists of precepts. These are not rules, but training guidelines. They are guidelines for skilful living. Until we are fully enlightened like the Buddha we will act unskilfully, at least some of the time, so learning to act more skilfully is a practice and a matter of training.

The five precepts described below are one of the most fundamental sets of precepts. They are often given in a negative form, as in abstention from something unskilful. However, they can also be described in a positive form, as in what is skilful, and this is perhaps more important for our practice. It is usually more inspiring to think in terms of practising some virtue, than what we should not be doing.

(1) Abstention from Taking Life and Practising Loving Kindness

The intention of not killing and practising loving kindness is straightforward in principle. A mental state that wishes to deprive another of his or her life is painful and clearly unskilful. Conversely, a mind full of kindness is pleasurable and skilful. However, how we put this precept into practice may be less straightforward. Good intentions are not enough; wisdom is also needed. As we enter the ambiguous and complex world we inhabit, how we practise the precepts requires skill and judgement, as well as a sense of consequences that may be difficult to discern.

We may feel clear that we should never kill someone, but some would argue that there might be an occasion when to do so would benefit many beings. A dangerous argument with room for much rationalization, but some might nevertheless in good conscience make a case for it. In practice, most of us may not ever be in a position where we have to make such a choice. However, every day we have choices about the food we eat. Many Buddhists are vegetarian to avoid supporting the killing of animals, but by no means all Buddhists are. Some Buddhists take the principle further by becoming vegan, which includes avoiding all dairy products, since the dairy industry often involves cruel practices and killing the cow's off-spring. The dairy cow is made pregnant each year to ensure continued lactation and many of the offspring used for beef or veal.[5]

How great the range of life in which we practise the principle of non-violence is another matter of judgement. As a keen gardener, I struggle both over how to respond to snails that munch prized plants I grow and what to do with greenfly. Talking to other Buddhist gardeners, some tell me they will go to great lengths to avoid killing snails with any amount of copper rings, eggshells and sundry other measures. Others will resort to pellets.

In the UK most Buddhists would probably choose not to work in the armaments industry. Indeed, becoming a Buddhist has led some people to leave the armed forces. However, for a Buddhist in India from a poor background, work in an armaments factory may be the only way to support his or her family. Even if we don't work directly within an area that is directly involved in killing, we still have choices about how we use our money. Investing in the tobacco industry may bring in much needed returns on our investments, but such investment also promotes a habit, especially with aggressive marketing in developing countries, that leads to premature deaths.

How we respond to these ethical issues to some extent will depend on how strongly we feel about a particular issue, and is likely to change over time. Buddhism invites us to explore these areas and be open to the effects of our actions and choices on our minds. As we become more receptive, we may find that our ethical sensibility becomes more refined and actions that in the past seemed okay, start to become more and more uncomfortable and unpleasant. We might notice this change, for example, when we lose our temper with someone. We justify our irritability and scarcely feel it as an unpleasant mental state, but then with increasing mindfulness we may find it begins to disturb us and becomes a habit that we no longer want to feed.

As our ethical sensibility becomes more acute, we may notice more opportunities for practising the positive side of the precept. Almost any interaction with another human offers the chance to be kind. This includes simple things such as helping someone with a child in a pushchair down some stairs or appreciating people for their fine qualities with a little card. How we hold people in mind will affect our behaviour. At work, in particular, it can be easy to get into a polarizing them-and-us situation, with other colleagues or other parts of the organization. We can get caught up in feeling that we are entirely right and they are completely wrong. Letting this go and cultivating kindness in our minds can lead to finding ways to co-operate rather than oppose or moan, without us needing to lose our faculty for discernment.

As the ramifications of practising non-violence and kindness become clearer and more urgent we may find we may find we want to make bigger changes in our lives. Making such changes can be painful at least in the short term, since there is usually a conflict between our old self and our new emerging aspirations.

Tom was a bright, competitive young man who had always wanted to make lots of money. He started working as a city financier and was soon earning a high salary with promises of big bonuses and promotions. He worked long hours in an adrenalized environment and then partied at the weekend with his girlfriend who shared similar values. Despite his worldly success something nagged at him and he found that he was not as happy as he felt he should be. Tom had travelled in Southeast Asia as a student. Although he had spent most of his time on the beach or following other outdoor activities, he had been intrigued by the statues of Buddhas and the Buddhist monks he had seen. He had thought about reading more about Buddhism but never got around to it. He then decided to act on this and signed up for a Buddhist meditation course. On the course he learned about Buddhist ethics. The Buddhist values resonated with him and he found the meditation beneficial, however he felt increasingly unhappy with his lifestyle. After some time and much wrestling with this in his mind, he decided to leave his job. His girlfriend, unhappy with his decision, left him. His friends found his action incomprehensible. Tom felt alone and miserable, but in his heart he knew he had made the right choice. He started working for a charity raising money for disadvantaged people in developing countries. He found a new lease of life and sense of freedom as he put his talent and energies into making money for a cause that was in line with his values.

Although Tom remained in the business of making money, he moved from a line of work that was predominantly exploitative with little room for kindness, into work that promoted the well-being of others. Tom experienced this change in work as a move from seeing people as objects who could enable one to make money or not — almost the antithesis of non-violence — to seeing people as people, and money as a means to support their humanity.

(2) Abstention from Taking the Not-given and Practising Generosity

The negative form of the first precept covers depriving a being of their life. The second precept is about desisting from taking anything else from someone that they don't wish to give. Stealing in all its forms is the most obvious example, but this precept also includes appropriating other things such as time or energy from others. Keeping people waiting for a meeting or dumping our litany of complaints on an unwilling listener are ways we can use others' resources that they did not wish to give us.

Dāna or generosity is sometimes considered the primary Buddhist virtue. Some descriptions of practising Buddhism begin with generosity. There is a long tradition of mutual generosity between lay and monastic in Buddhist countries. The lay provide offerings, especially food, and the monks teach the *Dharma*. At its best, this practice may spring from genuine devotion and well-wishing on both sides. However, without being driven by a skilful mental state it can become empty and formulaic. With this precept in particular there is a danger of mental states and actions drifting apart. We give out of mechanical habit, or worse to manipulate or with resentment. This is not generosity. Nevertheless, there is a place for giving, even when we don't feel like it, in a conscious way, in order to work on our mind. Just something simple like offering to make someone a cup of tea can overcome the inertia of a grumpy mind and shift us into a happier space.

The scope of generosity is limitless. One list includes giving material things, education and culture, fearlessness, life and limb, and the *Dharma*. The effect of regularly practising generosity is to move us away from small-minded, self-concerns into a bigger perspective. It helps us to consider others and to connect us with others. When I have been exploring this precept on courses with people new to Buddhism, I have often been struck by how many people derive greater pleasure from giving than from receiving. Partly, there can be all sorts of complex feelings that we may have about receiving (so I like to encourage people to allow others to give to them, rather than block others' generosity). Nevertheless, when I invite people to reflect on having given something thoughtfully to another there is real sense of pleasure and uplift in the room.

(3) Abstention from Sexual Misconduct and Practising Contentment

With this precept we take skilful living into the sphere of intimate relationships. The first two precepts apply to all relationships, but, because of the often charged and complex nature of sexual relationships, a separate precept highlights attention onto this area. Gross examples of sexual misconduct include rape and domestic violence. More subtly, it includes the semi-conscious manipulation that can go on to obtain sexual satisfaction. Sexual desire is a potent urge that can steamroll over a sensitive awareness of the object of one's desire. Abstention from sexual misconduct primarily means relating to those we are sexually attracted to or sexually involved with as other human beings like ourselves. Hence, we aim to relate to them with kindness, consideration and generosity.

In the sexual arena, in particular, there may be considerable divergence between natural and conventional ethics. Conventional ethics are partly the happenstance of individual cultures and partly ways of regulating sexual behaviour in a given society. For example, lack of reliable contraception may invite norms of sexual behaviour that is not necessary when such contraception is freely available. Similarly, the received gender roles of a particular society may affect conventional ethics. What sort of, and indeed whether one has, a marriage ceremony, are also largely a matter of conventional ethics, as are attitudes to lesbian and gay relationships.

> Juan was wary of religious groups. It had been difficult being gay growing up in his home country. The local clergy had told his mother that various medical problems in her family were due to having a homosexual son. Juan emigrated to escape these attitudes. He was surprised to find a Buddhist meditation group for gay men. He started attending and was relieved to discover that he could practise Buddhism without his sexuality being a problem.

Natural ethics refers principally to the mind states and intentions that we bring to our sexual relationships rather than their outward form. As Juan was to learn as he began to find out more about Buddhism, it was the quality of an intimate relationship that mattered, not the fact of being gay.

Contentment — the positive formulation of this precept — includes and goes beyond the consideration of whether or not we are sexually active. We aim for contentment either within our intimate relationships or as a single person. More broadly, we seek to develop contentment in all situations. Living in a fast, complex consumerist society often militates against contentment. Choice is often lauded as a self-evidently good thing. However, too much choice can bewilder, lead to anxiety — rooted in the fear that you haven't managed to make the best choice — and takes up time. As we seek to make the best choice in the shifting world of phone contracts, utilities and savings, we can expend a lot of time and energy.

Factors that promote contentment include simplifying our lives, reducing the number of possessions, and taking time out to live in a less hurried way. Retreats are an excellent way to rejuvenate and find contentment. A weekend in the countryside on retreat with some like-minded people, and perhaps practising more meditation than we do in our home life, can make a big difference to our states of mind. The more that we have experienced contentment through being on retreat, the more possible it is to bring something of that into our daily lives. Pausing between jobs for a moment or channelling the mind away from its habitual worries to an appreciation of the fresh spring leaves we walk past on the way to work can significantly enhance the quality of our lives.

(4) Abstention from False Speech and Practising Truthfulness

This precept takes the exploration of skilful action to speech and more generally communication. There is a separate precept for speech since we spend a lot of time talking (or texting, writing and emailing) one another. All the old jokes about thinking before speaking, point to how easy it is to let words slip out thoughtlessly. The Buddha said that we are born with an axe in our mouth, by which he meant that we can easily cause damage through careless speech. Equally, an impetuous press of the send button can create havoc through email. And with email, moreover, we don't have the face-to-face contact, making it easier to misinterpret any message we send or receive.

Blatant lying is the most obvious example of false speech, but more subtly it includes how we exaggerate or minimize our communication for particular ends. This is a great area to observe the mental states behind our speech. Sometimes, for example, we might embroider to make ourselves seem interesting or to be liked. We might slant our communication to get our own way. Or we might omit or stay silent for our own purposes.

Truthful speech is a difficult practice. It's not just a matter of speaking the plain facts, although that can be hard enough. We need to know our own mind and have a sensitive awareness of our mental states, especially of our motivations. We also need to bear in awareness the person we are addressing. Real truthful speech includes elements of kindness, generosity and wisdom — even, and perhaps especially, when we have something difficult to communicate. I find a good practice is to notice who I have chosen to relate something to in my mind. For example, when something is irritating me, I might start mentally griping about it. Usually, if I pay attention, I am addressing my complaints to a particular person who I have brought to mind. Often I have 'chosen' the person because I think they will agree with me or because I want to chide them or get back at them. Reflecting on why my mind has chosen this person and not another can bring insights into the mind states driving the urge to communicate. This act of reflection gives me a chance to avoid unnecessary damage and find a more skilful way to speak.

(5) Abstention from Intoxicants and Practising Mindfulness

Alcohol is the number one intoxicant in modern Western culture, but any substance that impairs awareness is included in this precept. Buddhists variously interpret the precept as meaning that one should avoid all intoxicating substances whatsoever or that moderate use is okay insofar as it doesn't cloud your mind. We need to look to our own minds to see whether 'moderate' use is reasonable or actually a rationalization to justify a behaviour we know we ought to stop. The disinhibiting effect of alcohol can lead to us being more likely to break the other precepts. Our boisterous humour may feel fine subjectively; it may take a non-drinking friend to apprise us that our speech was harsh and that the person who was the object of our humour was left feeling hurt.

The primary purpose of this precept is valuing mindfulness or awareness. We began our exploration of Buddhist practice in this book with mindfulness since a clear mind is an essential foundation. The more we practise, the more we notice the benefits of sharp awareness. One of my friends used to tease me for my habit of going to bed (and getting up) at a regular time each day. However, this was not born out of an ideological attachment to an abstract notion of it being good to go to bed early, but simply the observation from direct experience that, when I keep this routine (as opposed to staying up as late as possible during my student days), my awareness in morning meditation is always crisper and more flexible. I am more able to work with my mind, rather than feeling I am sitting in a tumble dryer!

Paying more attention to our mind we may notice there are other intoxicants besides the substances we ingest. Ones from the Buddhist tradition include youth, health and privilege. With these intoxicants, we forget the flip sides of old age, illness and disadvantage. Our awareness narrows and we can feel falsely inflated. As they are subtle, we may not find out we were intoxicated until we come down with a bump when their opposite arrives. Contemporary intoxicants might include shopping and surfing the net. Both can put us into an altered state in which broad awareness is lost and in which unskilful mental states can creep up on us.

Mindfulness as the positive form of this precept guards our mind. The more mindful we are, the less likely we are to fall into painful mental states through habit or circumstance. For this reason it can be helpful to make especial efforts to be mindful in situations that we know we are vulnerable in. Visiting one's parents or the supermarket for example might be times when habitual unhelpful reactions emerge, where a good dose of mindfulness can ameliorate trouble!

Practising the Precepts and the Environment

Concern for the well-being of our planet follows from trying to live skilfully and spans a number of the precepts. Having a large carbon footprint contributes to adverse climate change that can threaten life, whether directly through loss of habitat or indirectly through spread of disease (for example, malaria extending into new areas), increased malnutrition in poor countries that are less able to grow food, and making war more likely from conflict over scarce resources. Through taking more than our 'fair share' of the planet's resources we are also taking the not-given in relation to those we share the planet with, but who are less able to obtain a similar level of wealth.

Ecological concern can add another dimension to how we practise the precepts. Being vegan not only means not taking the life of animals, but also diminishes environmental impact since meat production consumes much more energy than eating plants. Practising simplicity and contentment may contribute not just to our own well-being, but also to reducing the adverse effect we have on our planet. Some Buddhists are therefore keen to reuse and recycle wherever possible, refrain from acquiring new material objects, as well as avoiding or minimizing air travel. Sharing our resources — whether that is letting others use our car or living communally — can also help to minimize our environmental impact.

Living skilfully requires that we reflect on the likely consequences of our actions. Compared to even fifty years ago, we now know much more about the adverse effects of our lifestyle on the planet, especially the contribution to environmental damage that can be caused by those of us with affluent lives. Change is, of course, inevitable — as the Buddha said, all things are impermanent. However, this is not an excuse for avoiding doing what we can to mitigate changes that threaten life on our planet. The Buddha appears to have cared about the environment — he appreciated its beauty and in small ways encouraged his disciples to look after it, for example, in how waste food from alms rounds was disposed of. He also intervened, when he could, to prevent the outbreak of war. Although it can feel that my individual action is dwarfed by the scale of the environmental problem and therefore hardly matters, our small efforts can nevertheless support a bigger movement to help alleviate the ecological troubles that we are facing.

CHAPTER 6

Taking the Teachings to Work

If your work is not your meditation, your meditation is not meditation.[1]
— Sangharakshita

The nadir came after I broke my arm. Cycling home from work one day I braked suddenly going downhill and with a faulty back brake did a forward flip over the handlebars. A crowd came to my assistance, gathering the groceries that had spilled from the bags hanging off my front handlebars, and calling an ambulance. Soon I found myself in the Emergency Department of the local hospital, calling home to let my friends know that I had a broken arm and that dinner would be a bit late. Afterwards, I continued as best I could with one arm out of action. I led a weekend retreat saluting the Buddha with one hand and back at work started to get used to operating a keyboard with a single hand.

Then a strange thing happened. I found my mind just refused to focus on the work I was trying to do. At the time, I was doing a research job and each time I sat in front of the computer my mind would go foggy, like I was swimming in treacle. This came as a surprise to me, as I had never experienced anything like it before. In the past, even when I was working hard, I had always been able to push through any resistance, and get on with the task at hand. Fortunately, I had a supportive boss and she let me come and go, doing what I felt up to. For a while all I seemed to be able to do was read novels; a computer screen and my mind would shut down. I just had to surrender to my incapacitated state. What did become clear was that I wasn't happy in the work, which had come to feel utterly meaningless. Either the work had to change or I had to change!

The Buddha's Emphasis on Right Livelihood

Many of us spend a lot of our waking hours working. If we include unpaid work, such as voluntary work, childcare or household chores, it adds up to a lot of time. If we are serious about practising the *Dharma*, we need to give some consideration to how we practise in relation to our work.

One of the Buddha's central insights was into the nature of conditionality. We are shaped and affected by the conditions we put ourselves into. We should not underestimate the powerful influence of the views and values of the people we work with and within the working environment. Around the time before I broke my arm, I noticed that when I was at work I would contemplate endeavouring to turn my research into a higher degree. Completing a doctorate and publishing papers was a major aim of the academic world I was in. With the motivation to advance my career, I would get caught up in those desires. Yet once I was away from that environment, my ambition would fall away. It was almost like I was two people depending whether I was at work or at home. Given the strong impact of our work upon us, it is helpful to reflect on whether these conditions are supportive of our attempts to practise the *Dharma*.

Yet although we are affected by our work conditions, in principle we are a free agent and can shape our responses to whatever conditions we find ourselves in. If we have enough mindfulness — and sometimes enough courage — we can notice the effects of our work on our mind and choose to respond in a skilful way. Indeed, because many of us spend so much time working (whether paid or unpaid), we have a great opportunity to put into practice the teachings of the Buddha. We are likely to meet similar situations again and again, giving us repeated chances to find creative responses to the challenges we meet at work.

Right Livelihood At the Time of the Buddha

Compared to urban industrialized society of the twenty-first century, the Buddha lived in a relatively simple, predominantly agrarian society. Nevertheless, he saw the importance of work for practising the *Dharma* and devoted one of the eight stages of the Noble Eightfold Path to livelihood. The main emphasis seems to have been on avoiding occupations that would lead to one frequently going against the precepts, especially harming other living beings. Hence, the work to be avoided included trading in weapons, trading in living beings, trading in meat, trading in intoxicants and trading in poison.[2] Apart from directly harming other beings, these occupations are likely to foster mental states of cruelty or, at best, indifference to the life of others. Such cruelty or indifference is the antithesis to compassion, which is one of the hallmarks of the awakened state.

In addition, the Buddha gave advice on how to conduct one's relationships with one's employer and employees.[3] The focus here is other-regarding and co-operation: how the employer can look after their employees and how employees can do their job well for their employer. Some of the employer's duties are to ensure that an employee has work that is suitable for them and looking after them when they are ill. The employee only takes what he or she is given and is the bearer of the employer's good repute — perhaps a different attitude from our sometimes habitual grumbling, where we can be tempted to blame the management as an easy target. I am reminded of the Chinese metaphor where hell is seen as a great banquet where you have to eat with very long chopsticks and each person tries to help themselves. Feeding oneself in this situation is tricky, leading to frustration as the tasty viands remain just out of reach. Heaven, by contrast, is the same banquet, but each helps feed each other. Co-operation ensures that everyone gets to enjoy the meal. As well as getting fed, there is the additional reward of participating in enabling others to be nourished.

Right Livelihood Today

Although times have changed since the Buddha's day and life is generally more complex, the principles still apply. For example, work that depends on child labour in unhealthy conditions is unlikely to be supportive of someone trying to cultivate compassion. However, what may be different from the time of the Buddha is that the effects of one's action at work may be more remote from the day-to-day working environment. Child labour may go on unseen in a country a long way from our own. We may need a degree of perspective and imagination to see and feel the effects of our work on others. Marketing and advertising industries may be involved in promoting greed for objects that we don't really need, even though the work itself has a degree of creativity in it.

The starting point for thinking about our work is to what extent it is line with and conducive to practising the five precepts, that is, cultivating kindness, generosity, contentment, truthfulness and awareness, and avoiding the opposite of these qualities. Doing work that we find inherently unskilful may well cause conflict and we may want to think about changing our livelihood (as happened with Tom, whom we met in the last chapter). In addition, our work ideally should be meaningful, perhaps giving something back to the world. Thus, our means of livelihood would be vocational — work that is consonant with our deepest values. However, it is not always as simple as having a job that has right livelihood written on the label. Although I personally have generally enjoyed my work with patients and found it satisfying, others working in the caring professions can discover mixed motivations that complicate their work.

Suzy had trained as a social worker and had worked for over a decade with people with learning disabilities. She felt passionate about the work, but also felt stressed in her working environment. To help with the stress she started going to classes to learn to meditate. The meditation seemed to be helping and then she heard about a weekend retreat for people in the caring professions. This seemed perfect: the opportunity to go deeper in meditation and to get to know like-minded people doing similar work to herself. On the retreat she did indeed go deeper in meditation. However, through the meditation and talking with other participants she became aware of deep-seated conflict. Although she did feel the work was important she became painfully aware of how much she was also driven by a desire to please. Her brother had a learning disability and growing up his needs had seemed to eclipse her own. The best way that she had found to gain approval as a child was to not make a fuss and help care for her younger brother. Suzy also had a creative side that she had mostly ignored over the years. Following the retreat, she arranged to work part-time and began a foundation arts course, with a view to trying to eventually find work in an arts-related field.

Some people have said, after completing a meditation and Buddhism course, that they got more than they bargained for! Developing more awareness and discovering deeper values can mean we end up wanting to significantly change how we live, and sometimes this can be quite disruptive to our heretofore seemingly well-ordered life. Suzy had no sense beforehand that she would end up wanting to stop working in her profession. Our deepening awareness may precipitate a crisis in how we live. Sometimes it is the other way round: as we peak in our career a midlife crisis may provoke us to look for something more. Practising meditation may help to guide us through this difficult terrain as we re-evaluate what is important, or the Buddha's teachings may provide a new source of meaning at this stage in our lives, which may affect how we go about working.

A consideration in contemplating right livelihood is that it leaves us with sufficient time for meditation, reflection, meeting with friends and other aspects of practising the *Dharma*. Suzy found an initial compromise by working part-time. We may have to take a long-term view on this, by doing something now that is important to us and practising as best we can in these conditions, in the knowledge that hopefully we should have more time later for dedicated *Dharma* practice. Bringing up children is an obvious example — not that this is incompatible with practising the *Dharma*. On the contrary, it offers rich opportunities for developing skilful qualities in meeting the objective demands of growing and changing children. Nevertheless, in practical terms, it is likely to be harder to get away on retreat or even to meditate for very long at home, especially when the children are young. At the same time, we should watch out for rationalizations that mean we just put off practising the *Dharma*: 'too young to meditate', 'too much schoolwork to meditate', 'too much in love to meditate', 'too much work to meditate', 'too old to meditate' and so forth.

We each have to find our way through the business of how to earn a living skilfully and to practise. The change I needed to make came to me gradually as I reflected while my arm was broken. I realised that I was learning a lot through the research I was doing and that seeing it through would be helpful to me in the long-term. At the same time, I clearly saw that I did not want to become an academic and that direct patient care had to be the main focus of my work, which is what I returned to after completing the research. Having 'down time', while my arm was broken, helped me to sift through my motivations to locate those that were in accord with my deepest values. Working directly with patients, most closely met my urge to help people — a central value for me. By contrast, if I had continued in research, the principal motivation would likely have been about acquiring more status. Making these sorts of decisions is going to be highly personal. For another person, being an academic might be a more fulfilling way of satisfying his or her most cherished values.

Some Buddhists have set up their own businesses in order to provide work that is ethical and meaningful, as well as to generate income that can be given to Buddhist causes such as running public centres that teach meditation and Buddhism. Often these businesses function as a team — team-based right livelihoods — where the close interaction with other people trying to practise the

Dharma can support and challenge. Mental habits that may be missed in the privacy of one's meditation practice can sometimes be seen more clearly and be transformed when reflected back kindly by other people who share one's values. Another way of gaining support to practise at work is when people from a similar occupational background get together to share their experiences. This might be an informal meeting or something more structured such as the retreat for people in the caring professions that Suzy attended.

Working Skilfully in Any Context

Whatever our work situation, it is always possible to put mindfulness, kindness and the other precepts into practice. A good place to start is trying to be more aware of our body and mind. We can pause a moment between emails and check our posture, sitting up if we find we have slumped. If we have to move between places, even if it is just to the next room, we can bring awareness to our feet as we are walking. This can take us for a few moments out of our habitual thinking, which may include worrying and be causing ourselves additional stress. We can take a breathing space (chapter 2) while standing at the photocopier or waiting for the kettle to boil.

Work usually involves other people, albeit perhaps only at the end of a telephone or email. There is a lot of scope for considering how we can be kind and helpful in our interaction with others. We can reflect on how to best co-operate rather than just trying to get our own way. Work situations often invite gossip. There can be a strong pull to join in to be part of the group. A real challenge can be finding ways to talk skilfully about other people or desist from talking about others at all.

If we work on our mind at work it will support our practice, especially meditation, outside of work. It can also yield rich rewards of making our work less stressful and more enjoyable both for ourselves and those we work with. This is likely to contribute to us being more productive at work and of benefit to others. A friend told me that one of her colleagues had commented on her calm presence at work and what a good effect that had on the atmosphere at work. She was initially surprised, since her inner experience was anything but calm. Yet she was able to recognize that by practising mindfulness at work she was managing her work better and this was having a positive effect on those around her.

Around the time I broke my arm, although my working life was painful, I don't regret having chosen to do that work or the discomfort that the work brought out. It forced me to clarify what was most important to me, which otherwise I might not have recognized so clearly. Work can throw up challenges that in other situations we might be able to avoid. If we can bring the principles of the *Dharma* to bear, we can meet those challenges in creative ways and really grow as a result.

CHAPTER 7

Friendship

*Ānanda: 'Venerable sir, this is half of the spiritual life, that is,
good friendship, good companionship, good comradeship'.
The Buddha: 'Not so, Ānanda! Not so, Ānanda!
This is the entire spiritual life, Ānanda, that is,
good friendship, good companionship, good comradeship'.*[1]
— Saṃyutta Nikāya 45:8; V 8–10

The Third Jewel of Buddhism: *Sangha*

Most iconic of all the images of the Buddhism is perhaps the Buddha seated cross-legged in meditation underneath the Bodhi tree as he gains awakening. However, it would be equally true to bring to mind the Buddha surrounded by disciples meditating together or teaching. A famous incident recounts King Ajātasattu, who has an uneasy mind having killed his father, being advised to visit the Buddha to seek some solace. He decides to go, but as he draws near to where he is told he will find the Buddha with a large gathering of disciples, he fears a plot for his own assassination. He cannot believe there could be a lot of people close by because it is so quiet. Persuaded to proceed, he reaches a clearing where the Buddha is indeed sitting with many disciples, all perfectly silent in tranquil meditation.[2] There is a stark contrast between the suspicion that Ajātasattu holds towards his subjects, and the deep peace and harmony between the Buddha and his disciples.

The *Sangha* is the spiritual community of followers of the Buddha. The term is used broadly to include any follower of the Buddha, or more narrowly to those with some degree of spiritual attainment. As one of the three jewels, the *Sangha* is one of the three key aspects of Buddhism and has been important from early times. The other two jewels are the Buddha (the exemplar of the ideal of Buddhism) and the *Dharma* (both the Truth of how things are and the teaching of the Buddha, which enables one to realise the Truth). Even though there was sometimes conflict in the early *Sangha*, we also get glimpses of real harmony among the first followers of the Buddha. A lovely example is the three Anuruddhas.[3] These three disciples lived together, looking after each other, meditating together and discussing the *Dharma* with real ease, co-operation and mutual kindness.[4] The quality of harmony between these three friends was a testament to the maturity of their practice of Buddhism. Following the teachings of the Buddha leads to the overcoming of self-centredness and self-preoccupation, so that harmony and friendship can flourish.

Sangha is important because teachers and exemplars of the *Dharma* are one of the best ways we learn about Buddhism. We also learn and gain support from practising alongside other people following the same path as us. As we gain more experience, teaching those with less experience than ourselves is a further spur to practice. The overarching aim of Buddhism is to help us move beyond our own self-preoccupation, which blinds us to the transient and interconnected nature of life, in order to give birth to wisdom and compassion. To go beyond ourselves, with all our myopic likes and dislikes, we need other people; we need the *Sangha*.

Gaining Guidance from More-experienced Practitioners

Having contact with people who have more experience in practising the *Dharma* can help us; however, this is not always straightforward, as in the following example:

> Joshua had been attending meditation classes for some months. He was enthusiastic about the practices and decided to go on a retreat. It was quite a step up and meant doing a lot more meditation than he was used to. There were also other activities such as talks and ritual. Each afternoon there was a group to discuss how people were doing on the retreat, facilitated by one of the senior members of the retreat team. Joshua felt uncomfortable in the group. He found himself unusually argumentative and wanting to criticize the group leader. Later in the retreat, during a period of silence he took himself off for a walk and tried to put into practice the mindfulness teachings that he had been learning, bringing awareness to his body and to his thoughts and feelings. As he walked, it began to dawn on him that what he felt most uncomfortable about was the idea that someone else could be more spiritually developed than he was, and that this was somehow threatening to him. He felt personally diminished and it challenged his cherished belief that all people are equal.

Since people are not uni-dimensional, it is not possible (and probably not desirable) to put people in a strict hierarchy from least to most spiritually developed. Nevertheless, the Buddhist tradition has described a number of stages of spiritual development and the central purpose of Buddhism is to move from a state of spiritual ignorance to full awakening.[5] Inevitably, then, there will be some people with more spiritual experience than ourselves, at least in some areas.

There are a number of pitfalls that can stem from this. One is that we can get caught up in working out what level of spiritual attainment a particular teacher has and worrying about how far we are along the path. This is sometimes referred to as *spiritual materialism*, a condition in which we try to add spiritual attainments to our relatively unchanged selves, like wearing some kind of badge saying 'I'm a very spiritual person'. Or we can get into 'my teacher is better than yours' attitudes — a sort of vicarious attainment. We can also be gullible, thinking that if our teacher has some spiritual experience he or she must be perfect in every way (an attitude that unfortunately some teachers have encouraged). However, just because someone has attained a real degree of wisdom into the nature of reality doesn't necessarily make them a good bike mechanic, or skilled at making business decisions or that he or she doesn't have any blind spots into the workings of his or her personality. Alternatively, like Joshua, we can fall into the trap of believing that people are all the same, which then means that we might be closed to learning from someone else's experience.

When we meet a Buddhist teacher we don't need to assume they have lots of spiritual experience just because they are wearing ceremonial clothing or have an exotic-sounding name. Our job is to try to be open and receptive. If they have more experience than us, it will reveal itself in time and it would be a pity not to benefit from their experience. This doesn't mean losing our critical faculties, but rather to take seriously what they say, weigh it up for ourselves, without letting a threatened ego block our receptivity. The more we are able to be open in this thoughtful way, the more we may feel appreciation and gratitude for any help we receive. This is likely to make us treat those with more experience than us with respect and kindness, which in turn should enhance our communication with them, allowing the teacher to reveal more of their experience.

Finding Support and Understanding from Peers

I don't remember clearly now our initial meeting, but the first time Maitreya-bandhu and I were on retreat together remains vivid: we clashed. At the time, he was finishing a fine arts degree. However, prior to that he had been a nurse, and with that came some suspicion of me as a doctor in training wanting to become a psychiatrist. From my side, I couldn't understand why he didn't like me. I was drawn to his perspicacity and his fresh, audacious communication. In the end, we did become very good friends, but not without a few bumps along the way and breaking through some of each other's semi-conscious self-views that we held.[6]

One such self-orientated view of the world that I had been unwittingly clinging to was that if I liked someone, then surely they should like me. In other circumstances we might have parted company after our initial clash. However, with the common reference points of truthful communication (the fourth precept) and the ideal of friendship in the *Sangha*, we continued to be in dialogue. Maitreyabandhu helped me by showing me some of my shortcomings, which supported and complemented my own practice of mindfulness.

We may start practising Buddhism with enthusiasm. The ideas are new and stimulating. We may have some 'beginner's mind' meditation experiences or notice beneficial changes in our life flowing out of our new practice.[7] However, sooner or later we will come across more ingrained habits that are more resistant to change, and then practising Buddhism can be tough. Maybe our meditation becomes difficult like we feel we are plodding and inspiration begins to wane. Friendships with other people who are practising like us can be a great boon at this time. They can support and encourage — and we can do the same for them when they are feeling uninspired. As we start to make changes in how we behave in our lives, even make some big changes in our lives, it is helpful to have other people around us who understand what we are trying to do.

Moreover, many of the qualities that we are trying to develop, such as generosity and truthfulness, relate to other people. It's easier to start to put these qualities into practice or put them into practice in new and creative ways with people who understand what you are about. In particular, trying to communicate in a new way can easily go wrong. I've had a number of clumsy attempts to bring greater honesty to communication that have backfired — the endeavour to be more truthful is much easier with people who share your values. One of the things that I enjoy in friendships (like with Maitreyabandhu) is the ability to be able to speak out loud in an unfettered way to clarify my thinking. He will give me the space to explore, and bring interest and his reflections to help move my understanding on.

The knowledge that is especially valuable is uncovering the views we hold about ourselves and our own habits. We need clarity on this in order to be able to grow, and yet it is an area that can remain remarkably hidden to ourselves. The opportunity to learn from disagreements, disappointed expectations and direct feedback, although uncomfortable, can yield great insights. Learning from difficulties like this is much easier where there is a context of trusting friendship.

Sometimes our habits only show up when we are in contact with other people, especially in groups, as happened with Joshua. It can be instructive to watch our tendencies. Do we feel competitive with the others and want to take over the group? Do we tend to go passive, perhaps psychically erasing ourselves, seeming to disappear in a group, due to anxiety or low self-esteem? Is our habit to agree and be compliant? Does the prospect of speaking up in the group make us feel anxious? When others talk a lot, are we relieved or do we feel righteous indignation? Often the habits that appear are long-standing ones that we may have developed in our families growing up. The *Sangha* can be a new 'family' in which we repeat (but hopefully transform) those well-learned patterns.

We can be curious about how we find ourselves behaving in groups and try to see if we can discover what the views are underlying our behaviour. Do we assume that people won't be interested in us or are we afraid of appearing not to know something, and so be seen as stupid? Is there a view that if we don't agree with people they won't like us? Do we feel that people don't really understand us and so we have to assert ourselves vigorously? If the group in the *Sangha* is working well, we may have the chance to explore these issues openly. At the very least we can use the opportunity as a source of reflection to gain a greater understanding of ourselves.

A network of friendships can also be helpful if we have strong meditation experiences or if difficult emotions start to unfold. The *Sangha*, including both teachers and peer friends, can help to provide guidance and support, acting as a safe container when unexpected events show up. Practising alone we may become overwhelmed by the deeper contents of our psyche.[8] Alternatively, we can become over-attached to our spiritual experiences and over-inflated, believing we have made more progress than perhaps is the case. Good friends and teachers can help to bring us back down to earth and to move on. They can help us to value what has happened, but without getting stuck in the cul-de-sac of self-inflation.

Reaching Out to Others

Once we start to have some experience of practising Buddhism, particularly if we are finding it helpful, it is natural that we will want to share it with others. After the Buddha gained enlightenment, he spent the remaining 45 years of his life helping others through teaching the *Dharma*. This is the spontaneous activity of the Buddha's compassion. We can emulate this by recognizing the suffering of others, especially where this is self-inflicted through not understanding how the mind and our world works. Even if we don't have a lot of experience, we can still be helpful to others. Sāriputta, who became one of the Buddha's foremost disciples, first made a connection with the truth of the Buddha's teachings after hearing a brief explanation of the teaching by one of the Buddha's newer and relatively inexperienced disciples.

On some retreats run by the London Buddhist Centre where I teach, a few of the team give life stories, describing how their lives have been affected by the Buddha's teaching. This may be the first Buddhist talk someone has given and yet often these are moving and can have a greater impact than didactic teaching. It is sometimes said that the *Dharma* is caught, not taught. Hearing about the lives of other people and how they have put the Buddha's teaching into practice can be inspiring and help us make changes in our own lives.

As well as benefitting others, reaching out to others can help us directly too. Firstly, when we explain something to someone else, it helps us to see what we understand and what we are not yet clear about. I have had some of my most helpful clarifications through trying to teach something to others. The other way in which teaching helps is by moving our preoccupation away from the fixation on ourselves. Sometimes it can be a relief to move away from our petty self-concerns or repetitive mental machinations. Beyond that, it helps us move in the direction of the Buddha's wisdom as we shall see in the final chapter.

CHAPTER 8

Ritual and Devotion

Bowing helps to eliminate our self-centered ideas. This is not so easy.
It is difficult to get rid of these ideas, and bowing is a very valuable practice.
The result is not the point; it is the effort to improve ourselves that is valuable.
There is no end to this practice.[1]

— Shunryu Suzuki

Steve had reached the point where he wanted to make a deeper commitment to practising Buddhism. After considerable deliberation he took the opportunity to make a public declaration of his commitment to Buddhism during a simple ceremony that took place in the context of a ritual called a *pūjā*. He invited some friends, who had no previous experience of Buddhism. After the ceremony Steve felt deeply happy. He caught up with his friends where he met with a mixed response. Some had enjoyed watching the ritual, but one was upset and another clearly angry. Watching him bow and make offerings to the shrine, they felt that he had given up his individuality and his intellect. Steve felt thrown and began to doubt what he had done. Reflecting further, he reconnected with the deeper reasons for his actions and decided to try to share more fully with his friends what the ceremony meant to him. It was a long discussion!

Steve had always said that he would never be boxed in by adopting any label or belonging to a group, especially a religious group. However, he came to see that he could call himself a Buddhist without feeling that he was limiting himself in any way. To his surprise, he found that by being clear about what he was about he felt freer.

The Language of the Imagination

The endeavour of Buddhism is a difficult undertaking. We are trying to gain enlightenment. To do this we need to transform deeply engrained habits. One school of Buddhism — the *Yogācāra* — refers to the essential transformation as a 'turning around' in the deepest seat of consciousness.[2] We are trying to move from a fundamentally self-orientated view of life to a larger, all-encompassing aware-ness. We are aiming to shift the default 'I'm the centre of the universe' perspective, with all its small concerns and graspings, to a wiser relationship with experience that is largely other-regarding and compassionate.

To do this we need to use our reason and intellect — but in itself that is not enough. We may well know in principle that something is good for us, but then fail to act accordingly. We need to find a way to speak to the deeper parts of ourselves, to engage all of us, if Buddhism is going to more than merely a good idea. One way of going about this is to engage our imagination. By *imagination* I don't mean fantasy or make-believe. I am referring instead to a deeper faculty of the mind that responds, for example, to poetry and music. When we are affected by a good poem, it reaches into us, moves us and shows us a new perspective.

Most forms of Buddhism have some elements of ritual. Ritual appears to have been part of Buddhism from earliest times.[3] In some cases — Tibetan Buddhism, for example — the ritual is elaborate and highly complex. By using the language of the imagination, such as symbol, music and gestures, ritual can help to bring our emotions in line with our aspirations more fully. It can boost our motivation to practise and help to engage in transforming our minds.

Negative Connotations of Ritual

Unfortunately, for many people ritual can have negative connotations. As for Steve's friends, it can have associations of giving up one's self-directedness. It may be assumed that it means blindly following someone or something, believing in something without any reason for that belief. Ritual can have associations of superstition, where rationality and the intellect are subverted.

The Buddha was clear that his teaching should not be followed just because he said so. It was to be tested against reason and experience.[4] Moreover, ritual should be engaged in purposively. The Buddha regarded ritual engaged in as an end in itself as a fetter. Ritual without active engagement, where we are going through the motions or doing it to tick if off the list, is counterproductive.

Imagining Enlightenment

At the time of the Buddha some of his disciples took to bringing the Buddha to mind when they weren't physically with him, as a practice. By recollecting the Buddha, they could dwell on his qualities and feel in his presence.[5] This gave them a connection to the goal and a sense of enlightenment that supported their practice. Over the following centuries new figures appeared out of the depths of people's meditation or through visionary experience, which brought out different aspects of the Buddha's enlightenment.

These figures are sometimes referred to as archetypal Buddhas. They are an important part of *Mahāyāna* and *Vajrayāna* Buddhism. Each one has a whole set of associations including a colour, gestures, a mantra (see below) and sometimes a whole *sūtra* or set of *sūtras*. Examples include Akṣobhya and Amitābha. Akṣobhya is a blue Buddha, who holds a *vajra* (a diamond thunderbolt) and is associated with wisdom, serenity and supreme confidence. Amitābha is deep red, usually depicted seated in meditation, and is associated with love and compassion. He appears in three main *sūtras* that are influential in Far Eastern, especially Pure Land, Buddhism.

In *Mahāyāna* Buddhism the ideal disciple is a Bodhisattva, one who seeks to gain enlightenment for the benefit of all beings. Archetypal Bodhisattvas are described as beings who are said to have completed, or almost completed, the path to full awakening after many lifetimes. Key figures include Avalokiteśvara, white, associated with compassion; Tārā, green, also associated with compassion; Mañjuśrī, tawny-orange, associated with wisdom; and Vajrapāṇi, blue, associated with energy.

Contemplating the archetypal Buddhas and Bodhisattvas gives us a way to feel into the qualities of awakening. The rich symbols can feed our imagination and can help to counter nihilistic views of the aim of Buddhism. By reflecting on these figures we can get a leg up to find a sense of the goal we are pursuing.

Bowing and Offerings

If you go to a Buddhist centre, perhaps to learn meditation, there is likely to be a shrine in the room where meditation is taught. The shrine may be simple or elaborate depending on the tradition. There is likely to be an image of the Buddha — a statue, called a *rūpa*, or a photo or painting. Often there are candles, flowers, incense and offering bowls.

The Buddha image is there to remind us of the human potential of awakening. It is a form of the ancient practice of recollection of the Buddha. People may bow to the Buddha and make offerings. When we bow to the Buddha, we are not bowing to a piece of wood (in the case of a wooden figure); rather, we are remembering the example of the Buddha and bowing to that potential — including our own — for enlightenment. It is both a sense of reverence and a recognition that we still have some way to go. We revere the Buddha since we see awakening as highly desirable and out of gratitude for what he did in gaining enlightenment and teaching the *Dharma* so that we too can follow his example.

Bowing is a mark of respect and represents spiritual receptivity. If we are not receptive, we can't learn. In some traditions, we may bow to the teacher out of respect and as the nearest we have in human living form to the Buddha. We may bow to each other, respecting each other as a fellow practitioner and as one with the potential to gain enlightenment.

Offerings are another means of cultivating respect, reverence and receptivity. The three traditional offerings are flowers, candles and incense. Candles symbolize the Buddha and the wisdom of awakening; wisdom makes things clear like a light shining in darkness; flowers represent the *Dharma*, acting as a reminder of the inevitability of impermanence; and incense signifies the *Sangha* — the fragrance of incense perfuming the air being like the effect of *Dharma* practice on the world.

If we have our own shrine we can adorn it with whatever is beautiful and significant for us. Often people find it difficult to establish a regular meditation practice at home. Creating a shrine, even just a corner of the room or the top of a chest of drawers, can act as a visible reminder of our intention to meditate. Giving some attention to the shrine, such as dusting it or putting on it some fresh flowers, can be a good way of disengaging from everyday activities and preparing the mind for meditation.

Mantras and Chanting

Mantras are sound symbols that are associated with particular archetypal Buddhas or Bodhisattvas. Probably the most well-known Buddhist mantra is *Oṃ Maṇi Padme Hūṃ*, which is the mantra of Avalokiteśvara. Thus, one can approach imagining Avalokiteśvara and the qualities he embodies either through visualizing him — a white figure with a radiant, compassionate smile — or through chanting the mantra (or indeed through both simultaneously).

The mantra is usually a set of Sanskrit syllables and is not directly translatable, although there may be various symbolic associations with parts of the mantra. For example, *maṇi padme* means jewel (*maṇi*) in the lotus (*padma*). Both are rich symbols in Buddhism. Jewels are associated with spiritual riches and the Three Jewels of the Buddha, *Dharma* and *Sangha*. The lotus is associated with spiritual unfoldment. When bowing or doing *pūjā* (see below) the hands are often held in the gesture of offering a lotus bud. *Oṃ* is sometimes said to refer to awakening in potential, and *hūṃ* to its manifestation in actuality. However, to focus too much on a translation is to miss the point. Tārā's mantra, for example, is basically a play on her name.

Principally mantras are chanted. When we chant a mantra we can bring to mind the qualities of the figure whose mantra we are chanting, or we can just focus on the sound. We can chant out loud or silently. A typical traditional number of mantras to chant is 108. This can be done while telling the beads on a *mālā* (or rosary) since Buddhist *mālās* usually have 108 beads. Chanting is a practice in its own right, but it can also be a good way to prepare for meditation, as it can help to quieten the mind.

Chanting is also practised with a verse or a whole set of verses or liturgy. Examples of the former include *Sabbe sattā sukhi hontu*, which is the Pāli expression for may all beings be happy; and *Nam Myōhō Renge Kyō*, which is Japanese phrase for homage to the lotus *sūtra*, an important practice in Nichiren Buddhism.

Pūjā

A *pūjā* is a set of devotional verses that can be performed alone but is often recited together with other people. *Pūjā* literally means worship, which can cause discomfort for people who have negative associations with worship in a theistic context.

When Suzy (chapter 6) first came across a *pūjā* she responded immediately. With her love of art, she was moved by the beauty of the ritual. When she was asked on a retreat to help make a shrine, she found herself completely engaged with the process. Subsequently the *pūjā* had heightened significance as she bowed and made offerings to the shrine that she had in part been responsible for.

By contrast Joshua (chapter 7) struggled with *pūjā*. To begin with he quietly avoided it. For him, it was too much of smells, bells and superstition. He disliked the idea of bowing to anything or anyone. Nevertheless, he knew that it wasn't a matter of bowing to some creator god, and that, in any case, it was entirely optional. Then, after he had had the realization that a lot of his discomfort on retreat stemmed from a view that everyone should be equal, since he felt diminished by the idea of anyone being more advanced than him, he decided to give *pūjā* a go. Although he didn't feel much during the *pūjā*, he did his best to engage with the meaning of the verses. At the very end of the *pūjā* there was a period of silence. To his surprise, Joshua found himself transported into a deeper state of stillness than he had ever experienced in meditation.

Some of the most beautiful and inspiring verses of *pūjā* come from Śāntideva's *Bodhicaryāvatāra*.[6] In the context of *pūjā*, worship is about opening ourselves up to the qualities of the Awakened Mind, in order that we too can move towards awakening. The *pūjā* unfolds like a drama in which in our imagination we move from our present state to full enlightenment. To do this we need to be receptive to and to feel appreciative of the spiritual ideal — hence worship. During the *pūjā* there may be verses to acknowledge our shortcomings or what holds us back, ones in which we commit ourselves to practising the *Dharma* and others in which we ask for teachings. Finally, there may be verses in which we dedicate any benefits we have gained for the welfare of all beings.

During a *pūjā*, as well as verses, there may be readings, chanting of mantras and the opportunity to make offerings to the shrine. Like meditation, *pūjā* is a practice. If our mind is not engaged it becomes a fetter. When we can engage fully we may enjoy its beauty, as Suzy did, or find, as Joshua did, that it can have a strong effect on our mind.

CHAPTER 9

Buddhism and Psychotherapy

'I feel I have been given an experience of applying a new set of tools that I can reach for both in times of crises and in daily routine. These tools are simple yet effective — and have moved me beyond moments of despair and helplessness — in the face of recurring depression. The sitting meditation has opened my eyes to the transitory nature of my mental states in a way I've not experienced before. . . . Personally it's been helpful that the course has avoided explicit Buddhist terminology and stuck to urban realities!'[1]
    —Feedback from a participant on a 'meditation for depression' course

Mindfulness for Mental Health

Shirley (chapter 4) first attended a Buddhist centre to learn mindfulness meditation to help with her depression, like the participant quoted above. Over the last decade, there has been an explosion of interest in Western Europe and North America in using mindfulness meditation to help with mental health problems. Some, like Shirley, may go on to develop an interest and deeper involvement with Buddhism; others will just learn the techniques to help them manage a particular problem such as depression or chronic pain. Mindfulness lends itself as a practical approach to mental health and other problems that can be taught in a secular way.

    The use of mindfulness as a therapeutic modality was pioneered by Jon Kabat-Zinn.[2] The course he developed is called Mindfulness-Based Stress Reduction (MBSR) and is helpful for chronic pain and anxiety. MBSR may also be helpful for other conditions such as psoriasis, fibromyalgia, chronic fatigue and stress associated with cancer.[3] It has been adapted for the treatment of recurrent depression (Mindfulness-Based Cognitive Therapy, MBCT),[4] and appears to be promising in preventing relapse into addictive behaviours, for eating disorders and for improving relationships.[5]

> Luca had been dependent on heroin for ten years before he sought treatment for his addiction. He was given a prescription of methadone and over a period of months his life became more stable: he was getting on better with his partner and children, and started doing some casual work. Although, in

general, his relationships with his family were improved, at times he would have outbursts of anger. Sometimes he felt like the slightest thing could set him off. When he was feeling like this he would get strong craving for heroin, which he knew would calm him down. He had a few lapses, but although he felt better in the moment, it led to more arguments with his partner and he felt disappointed in himself.

His treatment centre was running a mindfulness course and he decided to give that a try. As he watched his mind in meditation, he discovered that irritation often followed on from when he was feeling misunderstood or not getting his own way. He saw that at home he felt his family didn't appreciate how much of a struggle it was for him to stay off heroin and how hard he was trying. It felt to him like they took the changes he had made for granted and expected even more. He also came to see how defensive he could be, easily feeling criticized, and how he had unconsciously assumed that once he stopped using heroin his life would be without difficulties.

Gradually he learned to identify the triggers to his anger and stay with the discomfort associated with them. He sat in meditation feeling the painfulness of recalling when he didn't get his own way — for example, when his teenage daughter was being distant or argumentative. Sometimes anger would flash up in his mind, but he would watch it boil up and then subside as he continued to pay attention to the sensations associated with the pain underlying the anger. As he practised this in sitting meditation, he started to catch these reactions when they were happening at home and let them pass without giving vent to his anger. He also found ways of communicating with his partner how hard he was finding it, which she was more receptive to, when he wasn't so irritable.

The Buddha recognized that a lot of our suffering is caused by how we respond to painful experiences. He gave the analogy of two darts.[6] Inevitably, we will experience pain in life, which can be physical, such as back pain, or mental, such as the sting of when someone close to us is angry with us. This is the first dart. However, often we respond to this in a negative way, in the former case perhaps becoming fearful that our back will never get better or blaming ourselves for picking up something too heavy. In the latter, we might react to someone's anger at us by getting irate back and wanting to take revenge. This is the second dart, which makes matters worse. MBSR and the other mindfulness-based approaches exploit this by teaching us how to stay with the first dart and not let our minds be carried away into creating the second dart. This was how Luca was able to work with his anger, which was for him the second dart, a reaction to painful feelings that he learned to become aware of and to stay with.

A typical course is once weekly for 8 weeks, often with a one-day retreat. There are three main stages, an A, B and C: developing Awareness, learning to Be with our experiences, and making wise Choices. The first half of the course focuses on learning to be more mindful of our bodies and minds, that is, developing Awareness (as we explored in Chapter 2). Once we are more mindful of our experience, we can then learn, in the second half of the course, to accept and open towards our painful experiences (which we looked at in Chapter 3). By Being with our experience in this way we learn to avoid or minimize creating the second dart. When we learn not to react to discomfort with unhelpful, automatic reactions, we are in a better position to see how best to act, that is, to make wise Choices. In the case of the painful back, MBSR might mean learning to pay close attention to the exact sensations in the back (A), letting go of any negative judgements about the painful sensations and staying with the sensations with a kindly attitude (B), and perhaps choosing to do some gentle exercise like a mindful walk (C). For Luca, it was seeing the triggers to his anger (A), letting go of his expectations of the situation and accepting the discomfort (B), which enabled him to have calmer and more helpful communication with his partner (C).

In the mindfulness-based approaches described above, mindfulness is the main part of the treatment, especially mindfulness meditation. In some other types of therapy, such as Dialectical Behavior Therapy (DBT)[7] and Acceptance and Commitment Therapy (ACT),[8] mindfulness forms a part of the treatment.

Buddhism, Mindfulness and Psychotherapy

Buddhism has stimulated considerable interest from psychotherapists, both in terms of the overlap between what psychotherapy is trying to do and the aims of Buddhism (we shall look at that in the last section), and as something that may be helpful for psychotherapists themselves.

Mindfulness may be particularly helpful for psychotherapists. It may enhance their ability to be aware of their patients, and to bring to sessions what Freud referred to as an 'evenly hovering attention'.[9] In addition, it may assist a psychotherapist to be aware of counter-transference — the thoughts and feelings evoked in the therapist by the patient — which is vital in many forms of depth psychotherapy.

Some Buddhists have developed their own schools of psychotherapy drawing on Buddhist principles. Examples of this in the UK include Core Process Psychotherapy[10] and Zen Therapy,[11] and in the United States Contemplative Psychotherapy.[12]

Psychotherapy for Buddhists

From Freud onwards, one of the strengths of psychotherapy is that it has built up a set of developmental theories. These describe how early events and relationships from infancy onwards (and in some schools even pre-natally) can affect adult behaviour and relationships. This understanding has been largely absent in Buddhism. Thus, sometimes psychotherapy can complement Buddhist practice, especially where there are unresolved issues that may play out within the *Sangha* (for example, in groups or on retreat), and so interfere with practising the *Dharma*.

Suzy (chapter 6) had realized on retreat how her career choice had been affected by her early conditioning and this led her to make some big changes in her life. However, she was still troubled and felt guilty for moving away from a caring profession. She entered a period of psychotherapy and found it helpful to explore more fully how she had been affected by having a brother with a learning disability. In the therapeutic relationship she found herself trying to please and take care of the therapist, which the therapist gently drew her attention to.

Suzy had kept up a daily meditation practice, but she started to feel more and more stuck and would often get headaches while sitting in meditation. At the same time, she noticed that she felt more critical of other people at her local centre. The teachers, who had seemed so helpful before, now seemed flawed. When one teacher mentioned in passing in a study group that she had not meditated while she was on holiday, Suzy couldn't help commenting on it to a friend in the group. The friend looked quizzical and ventured to ask if Suzy might be experiencing a little righteous indignation. Privately dismissing it, Suzy nevertheless related the whole event in therapy, but as she did so she found herself in floods of tears. As her therapist helped her unpack what was happening, Suzy discovered feelings of impotence and rage.

Over the next few months, Suzy kept revisiting these themes and her meditation — now too uncomfortable — became sporadic. Gradually, she came to let go of the need to be a perfect carer and to forgive herself for this. She was also more forgiving of others, especially the less than perfect teachers in the *Sangha*. Her artwork flourished and finally she found a new way of approaching her meditation that was less forced and more enjoyable.

Joshua (chapter 7) had made a stronger connection with Buddhism. He now generally enjoyed doing *pūja*. Nevertheless, in classes when the *Dharma* was being taught he often felt irritable. Joshua liked to ask questions and often had comments to make on what was being taught. Sometimes the teacher responded to his questions or comments, but at other times seemed to brush over or ignore them. When this happened, Joshua felt put down and would try harder to voice his thoughts. At the end of one class during which Joshua had asked a lot of questions, the teacher took Joshua to one side and requested that he gave other people more of a chance to ask questions. Joshua felt incensed and humiliated. He complained bitterly of this to another teacher who also sometimes taught at that class. She heard him out sympathetically, and then observed that Joshua seemed more argumentative when a man was teaching and wondered if the gender of the teacher could be significant for him. Joshua was generally feeling unhappy. Work was difficult; he wasn't getting on well with his boss. Maybe the *Dharma* wasn't all that it was made out to be. Surely he should be feeling happier not more unhappy?

For some time Joshua had been thinking of trying some psychotherapy, although he was somewhat sceptical of it. A friend recommended a therapist she had found helpful, so Joshua decided to go to see him. The therapy was stormy. Joshua found himself competitive and hostile towards the therapist. However, over time he began to see his patterns more clearly. He knew from his first retreat that he had difficulties with the idea of some people having more experience or being more developed, although he thought he had seen through that issue. What emerged with guidance from the therapist was how his relationships with men were influenced by the troubled relationship with his father. Although Joshua had had a good relationship with his mother, his father had been domineering and competitive. Growing up he had sought the approval of his father but easily ended up feeling invalidated and put down. Now he could see how this coloured his relationships with his boss, the male teachers at the Buddhist centre and with his therapist. Gradually, he was able to work this through in therapy and find more helpful ways of relating to significant male figures in his adult life.

Both Suzy and Joshua had developed patterns of relating to people, based on their relationships in childhood, which affected their responses to people in the *Sangha*. Practising Buddhism brought these unresolved issues to the fore. Psychotherapy enabled Suzy to continue to develop awareness of herself and her patterns at a time when she found formal meditation too difficult. For both of them, psychotherapy provided helpful skilled attention to their difficulties that assisted them to own and change their ways of relating to people, rather than blaming others in the Sangha for their problems.

Choosing a Therapist

Sometimes people practising Buddhism ask if it would be better to see a Buddhist therapist. In principle, it shouldn't matter as good therapists should keep their own religious or spiritual beliefs (or lack of them) to themselves and their own beliefs should not affect the process of therapy in a significant way. In practice, it can sometimes feel easier if you know that the therapist has some idea of what you are talking about when referring to your Buddhist practice. For this reason, some Buddhists chose a Buddhist therapist or a therapy drawn from Buddhism like Core Process Psychotherapy, or alternatively select a psycho-spiritual psychotherapy such as Psychosynthesis.

Probably the most important thing is that you are able to establish a working relationship with the therapist. A supervisor once said to me that therapy is like marriage: if the first one doesn't work out, then maybe you just picked the wrong person, but if it happens again second time round, you need to take a good look at yourself!

The Goals of Buddhism and Psychotherapy

While Buddhism does not have the detailed developmental theories produced by Western psychotherapy, it does have its own psychological theories. Buddhist psychology tends to be orientated towards ethics.[13] Whereas psychotherapy explores personal narratives and how they originate (especially in childhood), Buddhist psychology examines mental states in detail now and their likely consequences.

Psychotherapy explores why we are feeling the way we are; Buddhism looks at what we are experiencing and what the effect of this is on our mind.

Psychotherapy, when it goes well, can help us to understand our early conditioning and in doing so can free us from some of our idiosyncratic patterns that cause us trouble. Buddhism addresses itself to the general human condition: what it means to be human, how as ordinary humans we cause ourselves and others suffering, and how to liberate ourselves from this predicament. Both are helpful and can help each other. As we shall see in the final chapter, Buddhism has the more ambitious goal.

CHAPTER 10

Wisdom and the Big Picture

As stars, a fault of vision, as a lamp,
A mock show, dew drops, or a bubble,
A dream, a lightning flash, or cloud,
So should one view what is conditioned.[1]
— Diamond Sūtra

Finding Freedom is the Final Aim of Buddhism

Michelle attended a meditation for depression course (Mindfulness-Based Cognitive Therapy, MBCT) to help her with bouts of recurrent depression. She had struggled for years with bleak, low moods, which seemed to descend upon her for no reason and stop her life in its tracks. She was desperate to find a better way of managing her moods and followed the home practice of the course assiduously. At first she could not see the point of paying attention to her breath and body. Then painful feelings started to show up — anxiety and distress — and wave after wave of critical thoughts about herself.

Nevertheless she persisted. She kept returning to the body sensations associated with the difficult feelings and breathed with them. Gradually she came to see with increasing clarity the fleeting nature of all of her experience. Exploring what previously had seemed to be a fixed and unbearable block of distress, she discovered an ever-changing flux of thoughts, images, feelings and body sensations. The critical thoughts still appeared, but she found that she could ride the waves, watching them come and go. The more she practised in this way the greater confidence she felt at handling the contents of her mind and a new found sense of calm entered her life.

One year later Michelle was still practising the tools she had learned on the course. At times she had fallen back into feeling overwhelmed by her habitual thoughts and feelings, but each time she managed to see it through and come out the other side. It was the longest period in years that she had not been depressed. She found that she had a lighter relationship to herself. Her life felt richer and she felt more alive. Having an experience of the transient nature of her mind gave Michelle a taste of freedom.

The ultimate aim of the Buddha's teaching is to help us find liberation from the traps and habits of the mind, and the suffering these cause us. If it's not conducive to finding freedom from craving, ill-will and confusion or ignorance, it's not the Buddha's teaching. We find freedom through the wisdom that sees, on a deep level, the nature of the mind and of reality. The Buddha gave us a number of descriptions of reality that can give us a way in to developing wisdom. In this chapter, we will look at what the Buddha called the three marks of conditioned existence and conditionality.

The Three Marks of Conditioned Existence

1. Impermanence

The first mark, and perhaps the easiest to approach, is impermanence. Everywhere we look we find change. Our bodies age. Trees come into leaf and fall. Buildings decay and new ones are built. Our thoughts and feelings change moment by moment. Someone dies and a baby is born. The seas are in restless movement. We know the whole cosmos — mountains, continents, stars and whole galaxies — is in flux, even if we don't experience it directly.

We know this, but we don't know it very deeply. Our minds have the habit of imputing permanence. I was on retreat in New Zealand, writing about some of my reflections. The sun was shining and in the back of my mind I said to myself 'oh great, it's a sunny day'. Clouds soon appeared and I immediately thought, 'oh no, another wet day'. When the sun came out again and I caught my mind imputing a perfect day, I stopped writing and smiled at myself. I asked myself, since when had weather been unchanging, especially in this part of New Zealand where you could watch the weather fronts arrive and white clouds vanish into blue sky? I was doing 'profound' reflection, while the rest of my psyche was busily assuming permanence.

The more deeply we can see impermanence, feel it in our bones, the less we will be caught out by change. Instead of fighting against it, we can flow with it. We can be alive to creative opportunities and live our lives with more equipoise. As Michelle discovered, seeing the impermanent nature of our mind can lead to a sense of ease and freedom.

2. Insubstantiality

Two Truths: Relative and Ultimate

We tend in everyday life to think of the world as being made up of separate, independent objects. For ease of communication, language uses nouns to describe phenomena with relative stability. We talk about trees and birds, people and the sea. The ordinary use of language to describe comparatively enduring aspects of our experience is referred to in Buddhism as relative truth. Most of the time the relative truth serves us well. It enables us to go about our daily lives, to recognize each other and the objects that we interact with in the world.

However, we can end up thinking, feeling and behaving as though experiences are more permanent and substantial than they actually are. It is like we get beguiled by language and in conceptualizing our ever changing world, for practical utility, as one of fixed, separate objects, we come to believe that objects have some substantial existence and we act as though this was truly the state of reality. On the contrary, according to Buddhist teaching, since everything is in a state of flux, nothing whatsoever has a fixed core or abiding essence. This lack of an enduring essence is the second mark of conditioned existence, called insubstantiality, and is the corollary of impermanence. The understanding of phenomena as being insubstantial and without a fixed core — despite superficial appearances of stability — is termed ultimate truth.

In particular, the Buddha taught that we tend to believe that we have a core within us, a self, which is the owner of our experience. We may then try to protect and defend this sense of self, or grasp onto the self. This sense of self may show up more strongly at certain times such as when we are anxious, for example. Perhaps we might go into a room of people that we don't know and feel that all eyes are upon us and judging us, even though they are mostly absorbed in talking with one another. Sometimes, when people disagree with us, such as when debating with someone from a different political persuasion, we may be upset or angry, not necessarily just because of the content of their argument, but because it threatens our sense of self. Times like this can give us an inkling of rigid, separate sense of self, which we tend to cling to, and which the Buddha suggested was an unhelpful interpretation of our experience or belief.

Misunderstandings of Insubstantiality

This 'corelessness' or lack of a fixed essence is often referred to by Buddhists as *non-selfhood*. The state of understanding and of being in harmony with this realization is called *egolessness*. Both of these terms can cause problems if not understood correctly. Non-selfhood does mean that we have no sense of ourselves as agent who can make choices and act on an everyday level. Sometimes — usually through difficult childhood experiences — people have a weak sense of their own identity or feel fragmented. They may also have feelings of inner emptiness. Hearing about non-selfhood, they can mistake their own inner poverty for true egolessness. Another misunderstanding is that egolessness represents some kind of regression, like going back to the womb or to the condition of a pre-verbal infant. However, reading about the life of the Buddha one gets a definite impression of a man with a strong individuality and a clear sense of himself. Rather than a regression, egolessness refers to a state of human development beyond our usual understanding of an integrated adult.

To clarify the difference between egolessness and deficits in ordinary psychological development, some writers have talked about needing to have an ego or self before you go beyond it (or dispose of it). This is only partially true. Healthy ego development certainly is helpful for practising the *Dharma*. However, egolessness is more like a different dimension, and one doesn't have to have a perfectly integrated self to make significant spiritual progress.

A further misunderstanding of the teaching of non-selfhood is the notion that because we don't have a 'self', a Buddhist should not stand up for him or herself or take care of oneself. This is to confuse the relative with the ultimate truth. From the perspective of relative truth, we have a self and we need to look after ourselves with kindness. The ultimate truth, when realized, helps us to let go of unhelpful ways of relating to ourselves, which tend to cause ourselves and others suffering.

The Nature of Egolessness

Probably the simplest way of describing what egolessness looks like is in terms of being less selfish. The more deeply that we see we live in a fluid world, the less we try to grasp, hold on to and control what we think of as mine. As we gradually let go of a rigid and separate sense of self, we may experience more fully our connectedness with other people and indeed with all of life. In recognizing more fully that we are part of an interdependent universe, we may respond with kindness to others just as much as towards ourselves. Making a hard distinction between self and other becomes less meaningful. Instead, we act beneficially wherever we can. This is an expression of the natural compassion of a Buddha.

3. Unsatisfactoriness

Whereas the first two marks are simply the nature of things, the third mark, unsatisfactoriness or suffering, is primarily the result of how we respond to impermanence and insubstantiality. When we try to fix things that are changing we will suffer. If we are expecting the weather to stay fine in a half conscious way — as I was in New Zealand — we are liable to be disappointed. Often we don't realise we are holding expectations of permanence until we are let down — we set off for the beach and it clouds over, the cat is run over or our partner walks out on us. We may then find ourselves railing against the universe or looking for something to blame, rather than coming to terms with how things are. Of course, it is natural that we will feel upset after a major change such as the death of someone dear to us. However, to the extent we haven't reflected on and recognized impermanence as an inherent aspect of life, we are likely to make it more painful.

> Barbara was in her late thirties when she was diagnosed with ovarian cancer. The news shook her; it was not at all what she had been expecting. She had never previously been seriously ill and had always taken good care of her physical health through her diet and exercise. Her parents were still well and active in their seventies, and no one else in the family had had cancer. Barbara had been attending her local Buddhist centre for a number of years and she redoubled her meditation practice to prepare her mind for the treatment to come.
>
> It all happened quickly. Barbara was soon in hospital having both her ovaries and her womb removed, and then she started receiving chemotherapy. The doctors told her she had a good prognosis, but for the first time in her

life, Barbara *knew* that she was going to die — if not from this cancer, then at some point. In practising Buddhism she had reflected before on impermanence and the inevitability of death, but this brush with mortality made it much more real. As she went through the treatment, a lot of her effort was spent in being patient with her body, bringing kindness to the uncomfortable sensations from the surgery and the chemotherapy.

With a clear sense of her own mortality, Barbara felt that had come to terms with the worst of the illness. However, she found as the weeks and months passed, she kept running into new areas of distress and grief. It felt like she was having to shed layer after layer, peeling back more of the views about herself, which she scarcely knew she had been holding. Her practice seemed to be one of letting go again and again. She had to let go of her ideas that she might have a child, and her view of her womanhood based on a complete, healthy and fertile body. Again and yet again, she had to face her thoughts that life wasn't fair, that this shouldn't be happening to her, especially given how she had looked after her body. She also had to come to terms with the responses of her friends. Some of them were great and very supportive, but others seemed to shy away from her, as though they were scared of her cancer. When this happened Barbara felt like she wasn't fully human. Each time she hit another area of upset, she would try to breathe into it, allow the waves of grief to pass through her and the tears to fall.

Gradually Barbara became accustomed to meeting the painful thoughts and feelings that arose. As the chemotherapy came to an end, she began to feel a new inner strength, even though her body was still weak. She seemed to be able to hold her views about herself and other people, and her expectations, much more lightly and this brought a kind of spaciousness and joy to her life, even when she was struggling.

We create a sense of selfhood through the stories we tell ourselves about ourselves. 'I am this sort of person', 'I like this, I don't like that'. All those conversations we have with other people, comparing our preferences, are a way that we fix a sense of our self. Although our tastes may change over time, it seems that we engender a sense of self from moments of experience — tagged with an 'I' or 'me' — stitched together over time to produce a feeling of coherence, rather like a movie creates a sense of continuous motion from a series of still frames.[2] Barbara's experience of a serious illness highlighted and shook up her sense of self. By working with her reactions, she was able to loosen her fixed sense self and so release some of the suffering that it caused. As an experiment, some friends of mine explored the experience of their sense of self by swapping clothes and food preferences for a day (they were the same gender and roughly the same body build). They put on each other's clothes and had for breakfast what the other person would normally eat. Just a day of that they found unsettling. The clothes we choose and the choices we make about what we eat all build a sense of a seemingly permanent selfhood. We identify too with our various roles as spouse, sibling, parent, or the work we do. One of the reasons why retirement or the children leaving home can be painful is that we are losing something we over-identified with. We feel that we are losing a part of us. In reality, it was just a label that we put on as a way of relating at a particular point in time, but through repeated usage we come to believe that this is us. The greater we have bolstered up our sense of self through the role, the greater the pain will be when it changes.

The fact that all things are impermanent and insubstantial can give rise to some anxiety. It means that we can never get lasting satisfaction from anything. Complete enjoyment is marred by the fear that we will lose the new phone or the weather won't stay fine or the person might leave us or change in ways we don't like. It's not that there isn't pleasure or that pleasure is a 'bad thing'; it is rather that if we pay attention we will notice in the background a slight unease at the fragility and instability of life. To realise the insight into unsatisfactoriness we need to face this unease head on. Rather than trying to push it out of our awareness or to control and fix things, we learn to live alongside this disconcerting fact of reality. We can then let go of trying to get more from things and people than they are able to give, and live with a deeper sense of satisfaction from being in harmony with how things are.

Cultivating Wisdom

The Buddhist tradition describes three levels of wisdom: listening, reflecting and meditating. The first level, listening, we hear and try to take in the teachings of the Buddha. It is called 'listening', because originally Buddhism was an entirely oral tradition. However, with the advent of the printed word, 'listening' may include reading a book or something on the internet. We are trying to understand what we hear or read.

The second level is reflecting, in which we turn over the teachings in our minds. We could do this sitting quietly in an armchair, or while walking, perhaps on a stroll in the countryside or in a park, or pacing slowly back and forth. We can also reflect through writing down our thoughts as a means to clarify them.[3] In busy contemporary lives, it is easy to neglect the second level of wisdom. We might make time for meditation and reading *Dharma* books, but sometimes it can be hard to allow ourselves to stop and just reflect. If we don't give ourselves this time, we are likely to spend our meditations thinking and planning. Although it can initially be uncomfortable to sit and do nothing, it is a practice that can yield rich rewards, helping us to clarify confused thinking and penetrate more deeply into understanding the *Dharma*.

Having reflected thoroughly on the teachings, we can bring them more easily to mind in meditation — the third level of wisdom. When our mind is more tranquil, we may be able to intuit directly what the teachings are directing us to. We may be able to see and confirm in our own experience, for example, the transient and coreless nature of the contents of our awareness. We may be able to watch closely how our minds create suffering and how to release the pain we cause ourselves.

The Underlying Principle of Conditionality

Another way of understanding impermanence and insubstantiality is from the perspective of conditionality. As the Buddha gained awakening he investigated how things come into being, change and pass away. He saw that phenomena don't just appear and disappear randomly, but do so in dependence on conditions. 'Dependent arising', 'conditioned co-production' or simply 'conditionality', as it is variously called, describes the process of how all phenomena affect each other.

There are many ways of reflecting on this principle. For example, if I reflect on the shirt I am wearing as I type this paragraph, I could note that among many other things it depends upon a friend having introduced me to the shop where I bought it, all the factors that came into me getting to know this friend, people at the shop who sold me the shirt, other people for having chosen this design, the people involved in transporting the shirt to the shop, more people involved in growing the cotton and others for making the shirt. All of these people came into being from multiple causes and conditions. As soon as we scratch the surface of any phenomenon, we find ourselves connected distantly or closely to a vast web of people and things — in fact, to the whole universe.

Yet although my shirt connects me to everything, some things are more closely connected and have a more direct effect than others (like the shop where I bought the shirt, as opposed to the person who designed the machine that was used for spinning the cotton that was used to make my shirt). The Buddha recognized the general principle of conditionality and in his teachings picked out key conditions that could help gain enlightenment. One example is the Four Noble Truths, which is an application of the general principle of conditionality to the problem of suffering. Craving, the Second Noble Truth, is one of the chief conditions for the arising of suffering. The Eightfold Path (the Fourth Noble Truth) describes important conditions that lead to awakening — the cessation of suffering.

Different Orders of Conditionality

Within conditionality we can discern different ways that things affect each other, that is, different orders of conditionality. Gravity is an example of a type of conditionality, describing a type of relationship between bodies according to their masses. Thus, we know that if we drop an apple on planet Earth, it will fall to the ground. Gravity is a general principle that we can rely on operating between the planet and objects on the planet.

The Buddhist tradition has described a number of different levels of conditionality. The two most important in the quest for liberation are the *karma* and the *dharma* orders.

Acting Through the Karma Order

Karma describes the effects of willed actions of body, speech and mind on our consciousness. Actions rooted in mind states of clarity, kindness and contentment will have a beneficial effect on us. Those rooted in the obverse will have an adverse effect. *Karma* is the principle behind the five precepts, which we explored in chapter 5. With careful attention we can notice how our mental states affect us. The more conscious and intentional an action, the greater the *karmic* effect is likely to be. However, habitual, often barely conscious, actions are likely to have the biggest influence on our consciousness, since such actions are repeated frequently. The more clearly we see the effects of our actions on our minds, the more we will want to cultivate skilful mental states. Over time this has the effect of making our consciousness brighter, clearer and more subtle.

Opening Up to the Dharma Order

Choosing to act in skilful ways can only take us so far. With a more refined consciousness we can reflect on the three marks of conditioned existence and on conditionality. Then we have to let go. We need to allow our reflections to work on us. This is sometimes spoken of as opening up to the *dharma* order. We cannot grasp after a deeper understanding of impermanence, because such understanding is not a possession. Or rather we should say there is no person, no self, that can possess such an understanding. Insight into the nature of impermanence, into reality has to come to us. This is a mysterious process. In the end, the Buddha's understanding, his wisdom and compassion, go beyond words. At best, the words can be like a finger pointing at the moon: they help us to see the moon, but we must not mistake the finger (the words) for the moon.

Conclusion

I started this book with the Buddha's advice to the Kālāmas: to try out any teachings in our own experience and against the testimony of the wise. When I first heard it, I found this advice resonated with me deeply. Over the years that I have been practising Buddhism, I have continued to find these twin tests helpful. I try to understand what the Buddha or one of my teachers is getting at, what the purpose of the teaching is, and then I check it out in my own experience to see if it can make a beneficial difference to my life. The Buddha was metaphysically reticent. He did not advance an abstract set of views about the nature of life that one should adhere to. Most of his teachings were method, rather than doctrine; that is, they were tools to help you change your life, rather than beliefs that you must hold. Even the ones in this chapter, such as the marks of conditioned existence, are primarily there to guide us into a deeper experience that can help liberate us from suffering.

My main endeavour in this book has been to describe the teachings of the Buddha that can be helpful for us living in the twenty-first century. Buddhism is rich with practices and guidance, which can make a real difference to our lives. Overall we are seeking to work creatively with our minds, and embody beneficial qualities, which we cultivate, in our actions and in our being. Meditation can help us to work directly on our minds so that we let go of unhelpful habits, which cause us suffering, and learn to respond creatively to whatever life brings us. The ethical guidelines can show us how to act skilfully in our daily lives and reinforce the positive changes that we are making through meditation. The wisdom teachings can help us to go more deeply into the mystery of being alive and lead us closer to full liberation. We aim to do this not just for ourselves, but also to benefit others. The book is an invitation to try out the teachings of the Buddha for yourself, and, I hope, to make a little contribution towards living more wisely and more kindly with each other on our small planet.

Notes

Introduction

1. *Kālāma Sutta, Aṅguttara Nikāya* 3:65, in *In the Buddha's Words. An Anthology of Discourses from the Pāli Canon*, edited by Bhikkhu Bodhi (Boston, MA: Wisdom, 2005).
2. Some of the vignettes are based closely on individual real people, some are amalgams of a number of different people, and some more made up to illustrate the sorts of issues that people face when practising Buddhism.

Chapter 1: The Buddha in Context

1. *Pabbajjā Sutta*, in *Sutta-Nipāta*, translated by H. Saddhatissa (London: Curzon Press, 1985).
2. For more on the life of the Buddha and its historical context, see Vishvapani Blomfield, *Gautama Buddha. The Life and Teachings of the Awakened One* (London: Quercus, 2011).
3. The term *Axial Age* (*Achsenzeit*) was coined by the German philosopher Karl Jaspers for a period roughly between 800 and 200 BCE. During this period widely geographically separated cultures simultaneously produced individuals who laid down the major spiritual foundations of humanity.
4. The *shramanas* introduced the concepts of *saṃsāra*, the endless round of birth and death; and *moksha*, liberation from this round. The *ātman* or soul was said to be reborn and move from one birth to the next. The Buddha assumed rebirth, but re-interpreted it by declaring that although there was a process of rebirth, no fixed thing such as soul moved from one birth to the next. For more on rebirth and how to approach it, see Nagapriya, *Exploring Karma and Rebirth* (Birmingham, UK: Windhorse, 2004).
5. Jains taught the principles of *ahiṃsā* (non-violence), *karma, saṃsāra* and asceticism. These were debated among different shramana groups and with the *brahmins*. The Buddha expounded his own understanding of these terms and practices.
6. *Buddhism* is a Western term that became popular in the nineteenth century to refer to the teachings of the Buddha. There is no exactly equivalent term in early Buddhist texts. Instead, these texts refer to the *Dharma* (teachings or the Law), *Buddha-dharma* (Buddhist doctrine), *Buddha-śāsana* (dispensation or

teachings of the Buddha), and *Buddhavacana* (word of the Buddha). Buddhism is generally considered to be a religion, although some prefer to see it as a way of life. Unlike some of the other main world religions such as Christianity and Islam, Buddhism is a non-theistic religion. The central figure of Buddhism is the Buddha, an Awakened human being. Buddhism does not depend on a belief in God, a soul or a supernatural being.

7. This was later also to be called a Bodhi tree.

8. The first teaching the Buddha is said to have given on this occasion is the Four Noble Truths, although his earliest teaching may have been less systematized than this. For more on the Four Noble Truths, see *Dhammacakkappavattana Sutta, Saṃyutta Nikāya, The Connected Discourses of the Buddha*, 56:11 translated by Bhikkhu Bodhi (Boston, MA: Wisdom, 2000).

9. Aśoka (269–232 BCE) was the Buddhist sovereign par excellence, putting Buddhist precepts into practise across his empire. His conversion came after witnessing the terrible destruction of his last campaign. He gave up all violence, promoted tolerance for all religions, built *stūpas* (monuments to mark places associated especially with the life of the Buddha) and helped to resolve difficulties within the *Sangha*. He documented his life and work in carvings on rock-faces and stone pillars: Aśoka's edicts.

10. For a fuller account on the spread of Buddhism, see Andrew Skilton, *A Concise History of Buddhism* (Birmingham, UK: Windhorse, 1994).

11. The eight stages or *aṅga* (literally, limb or member) are: right view, right intention, right speech, right action, right livelihood, right effort, right mindfulness and right concentration. See Sangharakshita, *Vision and Transformation: An Introduction to the Buddha's Noble Eightfold Path* (Glasgow, UK: Windhorse, 1990).

12. See Paul Williams, *Mahāyāna Buddhism. The Doctrinal Foundations* (London: Routledge, 1989).

13. Ambedkar converted to Buddhism and then led mass conversions of Dalits to help them go beyond the oppression of untouchability.

14. From *Upajjhatana Sutta, Anguttara Nikaya* (translation slightly amended) in *Numerical Discourses of the Buddha. An Anthology of Suttas from the Aṅguttara Nikāya*, V: 57 (1999) translated by Nyanaponika Thera and Bhikkhu Bodhi (Walnut Creek: AltaMira, 1999).

Chapter 2: Starting with Mindfulness

1. *The Dhammapada* v35, translated by Eknath Easwaran (Publication City: Arkana, 1987).

2. A Buddhist retreat is a period of more intensive practice, especially (although not exclusively) focusing on meditation practice. It is usually held in quiet rural surroundings to support the practice of meditation and reflection.

3. You can find an explanation of the four-stage mindfulness of breathing and be led through the practice at: http://www.freebuddhistaudio.com/browse?cat=guided_introductions&t=audio

Chapter 3: Working with Difficult Thoughts and Emotions

1. 'When the Heart' by Michael Leunig, in *Poem for the Day, Two*, edited by R. Bowen R, N. Temple, S. Wienrich, and N. Albery (London: Chatto & Windus, 2003).

Chapter 4: Introducing Kindness

1. *The Mettā Sutta*, in *The Sutta-Nipāta*, translated by H. Saddhatissa (London: Curzon, 1985).
2. Nicholas T. Van Dam, Sean Sheppard, John P Forsyth and Mitch Earleywine, 'Self-compassion is a better predictor than mindfulness of symptom severity and quality of life in mixed anxiety and depression,' 2011, *Journal of Anxiety Disorders*, 25, 123–130.
3. Stefan Einhorn, *The Art of Being Kind* (London: Sphere, 2006).
4. All experiences, physical and mental, have a feeling tone of being pleasant, unpleasant or neutral. We refer to this as the hedonic tone of experience or *vedanā* in Buddhism. Sometimes we may have a mixed response as when we have a conflict with a friend. If we examine our experience more closely, we may find it is made up of a number of sensations, some of them pleasant and some unpleasant.
5. For a remarkable example of someone transforming how they feel about a difficult person, see the interview of Marian Partington — 'Forgiving My Sister's Killers' — in *Challenging Times. Stories of Buddhist Practice When Things Get Tough*, edited by Vishvapani (Birmingham, UK: Windhorse, 2006).

Chapter 5: Living Skilfully

1. *Dhammapada*, verses 1–2, translated by Sangharakshita (Birmingham, UK: Windhorse, 2001).
2. Martin E. P. Seligman, *Authentic Happiness. Using the New Positive Psychology to Realize Your Potential for Lasting Fulfillment* (London: Nicholas Brealey, 2002).
3. For a fuller discussion on karma, see Nagapriya, *Exploring Karma and Rebirth* (Birmingham, UK: Windhorse, 2004).
4. *Moḷiyasīvaka Sutta*, in *The Connected Discourses of the Buddha (Saṃyutta Nikāya)*, translated by Bhikkhu Bodhi (Boston, MA: Wisdom, 2000).
5. Bodhipaksa, *Vegetarianism* (Birmingham, UK: Windhorse, 1999).

Chapter 6: Taking the Teachings to Work

1. Sangharakshita, *Peace is a Fire* (Birmingham, UK: Windhorse, 1995).
2. *Aṅguttara Nikāya* 5:177, in *In The Buddha's Words. An Anthology of Discourses from the Pāli Canon*, edited by Bhikkhu Bodhi (Boston, Massachusetts: Wisdom, 2005).

3. *Sigālaka Sutta*, in *The Long Discourses of the Buddha. A Translation of the Dīgha Nikāya*, translated by Maurice Walshe (Boston, MA: Wisdom, 1995).

Chapter 7: Friendship

1. *Saṃyutta Nikāya* 45:8; V 8–10, in *In The Buddha's Words. An Anthology of Discourses from the Pāli Canon*, edited by Bhikkhu Bodhi (Boston, MA: Wisdom, 2005).
2. *Sāmaññaphala Sutta*, in *The Long Discourses of the Buddha. A Translation of the Dīgha Nikāya*, translated by Maurice Walshe (Boston, MA: Wisdom, 1985).
3. The three disciples were Anuruddha, Nandiya and Kimbila. They are often referred to as the 'three Anuruddhas' on account of the close harmony between them.
4. *Upakkilesa Sutta*, in *The Middle Length Discourses of the Buddha. A Translation of the Majjhima Nikāya*, translated by Bhikkhu Ñāṇamoli and Bhikkhu Bodhi (Boston, MA: Wisdom, 1995).
5. Different traditions have different descriptions of the stages of spiritual development. Broadly, we can think of there being four main stages: firstly, an initial provisional interest in Buddhism; secondly, an effective commitment to practising Buddhism where your practice consistently has a positive effect on you provided you keep in reasonably supportive conditions; thirdly, a point of irreversibility from which it is said that is impossible to fall away from practising the *Dharma*, and enlightenment is assured sooner or later; and, fourthly, and finally, full awakening. For more on these different levels see, Subhuti, *Sangharakshita. A New Voice in the Buddhist Tradition*, pp. 92–94 (Birmingham: Windhorse, 1994) For more on different systems for describing the stages of spiritual development, see Sangharakshita, *The Meaning of Conversion in Buddhism* (Birmingham, UK: Windhorse, 1994).
6. For an account of this from the other person's perspective, see Maitreyabandhu, *Thicker than Blood. Friendship on the Buddhist Path* (Birmingham, UK: Windhorse, 2001).
7. When we first start meditating we may have few preconceptions about what should happen. This can give us a quality of openness and curiosity that sometimes leads to deeply calm and concentrated states of mind. The phenomenon is called 'beginner's mind'.

   Usually, these states don't appear again quickly, and the more we try to regain them, the more elusive they are.
8. I am using the term *psyche* here as a synonym for the mind, but with resonances of what depth psychology would refer to as soul.

Chapter 8: Ritual and Devotion

1. Shunryu Suzuki, *Zen Mind, Beginner's Mind* (New York: Weatherhill, 1987).

2. The deepest seat of consciousness refers to the *ālaya-vijñāna*, literally the storehouse consciousness. In the Yogācāra model the *ālaya-vijñāna* is a repository for the effects of previous actions, which may later manifest as the fruits of our karma. At enlightenment there is a 'turning about' or 'revolution at the basis' (*āśraya-paravṛtti*), in which consciousness, including the storehouse consciousness, is transformed into purified and radiant awareness. See Nagapriya, *Visions of Mahayana Buddhism. Awakening the Universe to Wisdom and Compassion* (Cambridge, UK: Windhorse, 2009).

3. Gregory Schopen, *Bones, Stones and Buddhist Monks: Collected Papers on the Archaeology, Epigraphy and Texts of Monastic Buddhism in India (Studies in the Buddhist Traditions)* (University of Hawaii Press, 1997).

4. *Aṅguttara-Nikaya. The Book of the Gradual Sayings*, I, 188, translated by F. L. Woodward (London: Luzac & Company Ltd., 1970).

5. *Parayana Thuti Gatha*, in *Sutta-Nipāta*, translated by H. Saddhatissa (London: Curzon, 1985.

6. Śāntideva lived around the 8th century CE, although *pūjā* certainly predates this time. For an excellent translation of his work, see *The Bodhicaryāvatāra*, translated by Kate Crosby and Andrew Skilton (Oxford: Oxford University Press, 1996).

Chapter 9: Buddhism and Psychotherapy

1. Feedback from participant on a meditation for depression course (Mindfulness-Based Cognitive Therapy for Depression, MBCT).

2. Kabat-Zinn set up a stress clinic in Massachusetts in the late 1970s. He worked particularly with people with chronic pain, for whom allopathic medicine could give no further help, as well as with people with stress and anxiety. Jon Kabat-Zinn, *Full Catastrophe Living. Using the Wisdom of your Body and Mind to Face Stress, Pain, and Illness* (New York: Delta, 1990).

3. E. Halliwell, *Mindfulness . . . Report 2010* (London: Mental Health Foundation, 2010).

4. MBCT has been shown to be effective in preventing relapse into depression in people with three or more episodes of depression. Z. V. Segal, J. M. William and J. D. Teasdale, *Mindfulness-Based Cognitive Therapy for Depression* (New York: Guilford, 2002).

5. C. Mace, *Mindfulness and Mental Health. Therapy, Theory and Science* (Hove, East Sussex: Routledge, 2008).

6. Bhikkhu Bodhi, translator, *The Connected Discourses of the Buddha. A New Translation of the Saṃyutta Nikāya*, 2, 1264 (Boston, MA: Wisdom, 2000).

7. Dialectical Behavior Therapy (DBT) was developed by Marsha Lineham for the treatment of people with borderline personality disorder. Influenced by Zen Buddhism, she uses mindfulness as a part of DBT to help people accept and tolerate difficult emotions and develop what Lineham refers to as wise

mind. See M. H. Linehan, *Skills Training Manual for Borderline Personality Disorder* (New York: Guilford, 1993).

DBT has also been adapted for use in addiction and eating disorders. See S. Evershed 'Treatment of Personality Disorder: Skills-based Therapies,' *Advances in Psychiatric Treatment*, 17 (2011), 206–213.

8. Acceptance and Commitment Therapy (ACT) was developed by Stephen Hayes for a range of mental health problems. He was not directly influenced by Buddhism and mindfulness, however he ended up with key parts of his model that are very similar to mindfulness such as being in the present moment and acceptance. ACT is open to drawing on any methods that are coherent with its model, and so many ACT practitioners now use mindfulness techniques in their therapy. ACT appears to be helpful for a wide range of conditions, especially depression and anxiety. See M. Webster, 'Introduction to Acceptance and Commitment Therapy', *Advances in Psychiatric Treatment*, 17 (2011), 309–316.

9. Sigmund Freud, 'Remembering, Repeating and Working-Through' (1914), in *The Standard Edition of the Complete Psychological Works of Sigmund Freud*, translated by J. Strachey (London: The Hogarth Press, 1960),12: 145–156.

10. Core Process Psychotherapy at the Karuna Institute in Devon was set up by Maura and Franklyn Sills. Their therapy is informed by Buddhist ethics and draws on a Tibetan understanding of the nature of mind that describes the mind as having three inherent qualities: spaciousness, clarity and compassion. In Core Process Psychotherapy, the therapist endeavours to be mindful equally of themselves and of the client, to help bring awareness moment by moment to the arising and changing process of the client. The therapist's attention partly on themselves is to discern counter-transference responses that may helpfully be offered up to the client. Transformation is understood to occur through bringing fresh awareness and perspectives to the client's habitual patterns, thereby unfixing them and allowing natural change to take place. F. Sills, *Being and Becoming: Psychodynamics, Buddhism, and the Origins of Selfhood* (Berkeley, CA: North Atlantic Books, 2008).

11. Zen Therapy was developed by David and Caroline Brazier of the Amida Trust and has its roots in Pureland Buddhism. In Zen Therapy the self is seen as a defensive construct. Consequently, attention is not given to building self-esteem or self-image as this is seen as counter-productive. Rather than attending to self-view, focus is given to engagement with one's life experience, as well as how one is living outside of the constraints of self-image. Grief and disappointment are inherent in the attempt to build a self. Facing these uncomfortable emotions offers the potential for transformation. D. Brazier, *Zen Therapy. A Buddhist Approach to Psychotherapy* (London: Robinson, 2001).

12. The Naropa Institute was founded by a Tibetan Buddhist, Chögyam Trungpa, in Boulder, Colorado. One of the courses they offer is in Contemplative Psychotherapy. A key idea in this form of therapy is that our essential nature — referred to as brilliant sanity — is already complete and whole. The essence of

therapy is to uncover this, rather than trying to develop something. The therapist aims to help the client stay fully with their experience and to investigate it. The main tools are mindfulness and *maitri* (unconditional friendliness) to first help the client see what is happening and then to help them stay with the experience. The therapist assists the client in cultivating their own mindfulness discipline. See K. Wegela, "Contemplative Psychotherapy: A Path of Uncovering Brilliant Sanity" (1994), *Journal of Contemplative Psychotherapy*, 9, 27–51.

13. Sangharakshita, *Know Your Mind: Psychological Dimension of Ethics in Buddhism*. (Birmingham, UK: Windhorse, 1998).

Chapter 10: Wisdom and the Big Picture

1. Edward Conze, translator, *Buddhist Wisdom Books containing the Diamond Sūtra and the Heart Sūtra* (London: Hyman, 1998).
2. For more on how we create a sense of self and its neuroscientific underpinnings, see Rick Hanson with Richard Mendius, *The Buddha's Brain. The Practical Neuroscience of Happiness, Love and Wisdom* (Oakland, CA: New Harbinger, 2009).
3. For more on ways of reflecting, see Ratnaguna, *The Art of Reflection* (Cambridge, UK: Windhorse, 2010).

Resources

Online Resources

You can download or listen to guided meditations by the author at:
http://thebuddhistcentre.com/practicalbuddhism

For talks, interviews and seminars on a wide range of topics:
http://www.freebuddhistaudio.com/

To find a Triratna Buddhist centre or group near you:
http://thebuddhistcentre.com/text/triratna-around-world

For retreats, including solitary retreats, in the UK go to:
http://www.goingonretreat.com/

Further Reading

Chapter 1: The Buddha in Context

Batchelor, Stephen. *The Awakening of the West. The Encounter of Buddhism and Western Culture*. London: HarperCollins, 1994.
Blomfield, Vishvapani. *Gautama Buddha. The Life and Teachings of the Awakened One*. London: Quercus, 2011.
Sangharakshita. *Who is the Buddha?* Birmingham, UK: Windhorse, 1994.
Skilton, Andrew. *A Concise History of Buddhism*. Birmingham, UK: Windhorse, 1994.

Chapters 2 and 3: Starting with Mindfulness *and* Working with Difficult Thoughts and Emotions

Bodhipaksa. *Wildmind. A Step-by-Step Guide to Meditation*. Cambridge, UK: Windhorse, 2010.
Burch, Vidyamala. *Living Well with Pain and Illness. The Mindful Way to Free Yourself from Suffering*. London: Piatkus, 2008.

Kamalashila. *Buddhist Meditation. Tranquillity, Imagination and Insight*, Cambridge: Windhorse, 2012.

Maitreyabandhu. *Life with Full Attention. A Practical Course in Mindfulness.* Cambridge, UK: Windhorse, 2009.

Mason-John, Valerie. *Detox your Heart.* Birmingham, UK: Windhorse, 2005.

Paramananda. *Change Your Mind. A Practical Guide to Meditation*, Birmingham, UK: Windhorse, 1996.

Chapter 4: Introducing Kindness

Sangharakshita. *Living with Kindness. The Buddha's Teaching on Mettā.* Birmingham: Windhorse, 2004.

Salzberg, Sharon. *Loving Kindness. The Revolutionary Art of Happiness.* Boston: Shambhala, 1995.

Vessantara. *The Heart.* Birmingham: Windhorse, 2006.

Chapters 5 and 6: Living Skilfully *and* Taking the Teachings to Work

Sangharakshita. *Living Ethically. Advice from Nagarjuna's Precious Garland.* Birmingham: Windhorse, 2009.

Sangharakshita. *Vision and Transformation: An Introduction to the Buddha's Noble Eightfold Path.* Glasgow: Windhorse, 1990.

Chapter 7: Friendship

Maitreyabandhu. *Thicker than Blood. Friendship on the Buddhist Path.* Birmingham: Windhorse, 2001.

Sangharakshita. *What is the Sangha? The Nature of Spiritual Community.* Birmingham: Windhorse, 2000.

Subhuti (with Subhamati). *Buddhism and Friendship.* Birmingham: Windhorse, 2004.

Chapter 8: Ritual and Devotion

Sangharakshita. *Ritual and Devotion in Buddhism. An Introduction.* Birmingham: Windhorse, 1995.

Vessantara. *Meeting the Buddhas. A Guide to Buddhas, Bodhisattvas and Tantric Deities.* Glasgow: Windhorse, 1993.

Chapter 9: Buddhism and Psychotherapy

Epstein, Mark. *Going on Being. Buddhism and the Way of Change*. New York: Broadway Books, 2001.

Kabat-Zinn, Jon. *Full Catastrophe Living*. London: Piatkus, 2001.

Mace, Chris. *Mindfulness and Mental Health: Therapy, Theory and Science*. London: Routledge, 2008.

Safran, Jeremy D., ed. *Psychoanalysis and Buddhism. An Unfolding Dialogue*. Boston: Wisdom, 2003.

Welwood, John. *Towards a Psychology of Awakening. Buddhism, Psychotherapy and the Path of Spiritual Transformation*. Boston: Shambhala, 2000.

William, Mark; Teasdale, John; Segal, Zindel and Kabat-Zinn, Jon. *The Mindful Way through Depression. Freeing Yourself from Chronic Unhappiness*. New York: Guilford, 2007.

Chapter 10: Wisdom and the Big Picture

Cooper, Robin. *Finding the Mind. A Buddhist View*. Cambridge: Windhorse, 2012.

Jones, Dhivan Thomas. *This Being, That Becomes: The Buddha's Teaching on Conditionality*. Cambridge: Windhorse, 2011.

Sangharakshita. *What is the Dharma? The Essential Teachings of the Buddha*. Birmingham: Windhorse, 1998.

Index